Art and Environment

Art and Environment

AN ART RESOURCE FOR TEACHERS

ARNEL W. PATTEMORE

VNR VAN NOSTRAND REINHOLD COMPANY

NEW YORK   CINCINNATI   TORONTO   LONDON   MELBOURNE

238767

Carita Peltoniem
Gr. 1 – Oakridge

Van Nostrand Reinhold Company Regional Offices:
New York   Cincinnati   Chicago   Millbrae   Dallas

Van Nostrand Reinhold Company International Offices:
London   Toronto   Melbourne

Copyright © 1974 by Litton Educational Publishing, Inc.

Library of Congress Catalog Card Number 72-9708
ISBN 0-442-26513-1 (cloth)
ISBN 0-442-29911-7 (paper)

Published by Van Nostrand Reinhold Company
450 West 33rd Street, New York, N.Y. 10001

Published simultaneously in Canada by
Van Nostrand Reinhold Limited

16   15   14   13   12   11   10   9   8   7   6   5   4   3   2   1

Library of Congress Cataloging in Publication Data

Pattemore, Arnel W
   Art and environment.

   Bibliography: p.
   1. Art—Study and teaching (Elementary)   2. Activity projects in education.   3. Learning by discovery.
4. Man—Influence of environment. I. Title.
N350.P28   372.5'044   72-9708
ISBN 0-442-26513-1 (cloth)
ISBN 0-442-29911-7 (paper)

Acknowledgments

The preparation of a book requires the efforts and the support of many people. A general concern for the human environment has been the stimulus for this book but the real inspiration has come from the children in our schools who truly represent our hopes for the future. It is their work which is used to illustrate the ideas expressed. We thank those children from Lincoln County and elsewhere who have interpreted their environment in a creative and personal way and whose visual statements are reproduced. They must remain unnamed but their work speaks for itself. Photographs are by the author except as noted.

We also thank Chris White who kindly read the manuscript and whose suggestions have been incorporated into the present text; Mrs. Agnes Clark who typed the original manuscript; Malcolm Binks who assisted with many of the photographs; Robert Martens whose creative evaluation of environmental forces has had an influence on our own thinking.

Especially would we thank Mrs. Dori Watson Boynton who has proven herself to be one of the most patient editors an author could ever hope to meet. Her work on the manuscript and illustrations has been extensive and efficient.

We can only hope that these efforts will help the reader to develop an art program that is relevant and imaginative. Art will truly influence our environment only as our school art programs are successful in opening the eyes of the child.

Contents

Penny Andonian

Introduction

Today's education is concerned with the child and with his total growth as an individual. Education through art concentrates on the creative side of the child's nature. Of course, the creativity each child possesses may be nurtured and developed in a great many ways, as is evident by the diversity found at any given grade level in different schools. We would like to suggest that one of the most productive orientations for the elementary art curriculum now is the person-environment relationship.

There is no doubt that environment affects the personality and the actions of the individual. And the individual in turn affects his environment. He comes in contact with other people whose actions he changes through association. He shapes his physical environment, molding it to his own liking. These are facts of human growth and development, and awareness of these facts would be a guiding principle in the planning of the art program. Indeed, such an awareness is a fundamental aim of education today and it will continue to be so for a considerable time to come.

Education reflects man's best understanding of himself and his world. As that view changes and expands, so does the focus of education. In the recent few years we have begun to see our lives—and our earth—in a new way. It is summed up by Donn F. Eisele, an astronaut and a member of the first three-man Apollo flight that orbited the earth for eleven days in 1968. He has said, "I was impressed from space with the wholeness of the earth, and I believe the human race is one whole thing and we should all be working together."

An environment-oriented art program would increase the awareness of the "oneness" of men, the "wholeness" of the earth. At different grade levels, different levels of awareness would be encouraged, following the natural development of the child. However, whether it is the young child who makes pictures of himself and his friends or it is the older student who plans visionary cities and futuristic activities, the school has a duty to make

The world of nature is important.

the student more aware of his environment and to lead him towards an analytical appreciation and creative involvement.

To become aware is to sharpen the senses and sensibilities. The art class is not only a studio in which visual statements are produced. It is an exercise in group living. It is an opportunity to work with others and to understand them. Art in education has many functions, among which must surely be the humanizing of students.

A child has pictured a stroll in the park.

Children will learn to understand one another as they see their work on display. They will appreciate abilities and help cure weaknesses. They will see that different people work in different ways and will learn to accept individuality. They will better appreciate their own abilities. But more important, they will learn about people by working with one another. Theirs will be a world where democracy becomes a way of life.

Art goes beyond the classroom. It takes the student out into the community where he finds subjects for his pictures and projects as well as an audience for the feelings and ideas he has expressed in his art work. With the broadening of horizons (and awareness), the boundaries and definition of the community are increasingly enlarged. In a sense, the community becomes the classroom and, ultimately, the world becomes the community. Thus, art and the environment are really the whole world as focused on the student creator.

Art provides an avenue for awareness and understanding of the world and, as the universal language, it is a powerful means of communication. Its possibilities are legion. In this environment-oriented approach, art instruction in the schools will explore many diverse areas, among them: the unique and universal qualities of the individual; the functional and aesthetic arrangement of immediate surroundings; mass communication and media and social comment; neighborhood improvement and town planning; the man-nature relationship and the challenges of ecology.

This book seeks to provide a general guide for an art program with environment as the central theme. There are suggestions as to the kinds of subjects suitable for the various grade levels and how to present and explore the ideas involved. There are also suggestions regarding media and specific projects. From beginning to end, the aim is to encourage a creative awareness, appreciation and involvement between each individual child and the world which is his life-long home.

An auto race is a source of excitement.

People, buildings, and cars all belong to the young child's world.

1 Groundwork

Children become aware of environment as they work together.

The purpose of education through art is to make students aware of their environment and more understanding of themselves and others. That this is accomplished through a series of practical projects does not detract from the intellectual implications of art education. With even young children there is an opportunity to relate art expression to intellectual growth and there is purpose to the picture-making activities. As we consider the environment in the art class, we want children to be more aware, to become more perceptive.

The school art program is always concerned with the environment. The pictures made by children are a reflection of their environment. The ideas that they express through their art are affected by the environment. Environment controls the materials available and suggests the topics chosen. Further, environment is reflected in the level of understanding and the degree of skill of each child. The challenge is to recognize the art-environment alliance and to make constructive use of it. To do this, the teacher must show interest and imagination, enthusiasm and empathy, energy and understanding.

There are many opportunities for environmental studies in the elementary art class. In fact, practically every art project explores the environment. The daily picture-making program draws on environment for its subject matter. Students will use their art to make statements about the environment they know and experience. Their awareness and understanding of the world will be heightened through such activities. Many special projects and integrated themes will be devised by teacher and class to make art more meaningful to the class.

In all of the projects undertaken, a positive attitude is important. Children should be encouraged to look for good qualities in their environment and discover beauty rather than decrying a proliferation of pollution. Our current concern with ecology will be reflected in the work of the art class but we do not endorse negative thinking. Rather, we hope to become aware of the environment and to consider its many dimensions in the contem-

Contemporary activities are subjects for pictures.

porary world of the young. We hope to encourage young people to understand each other and to look for innovative projects that will be aesthetically sound and that will make them more socially aware.

A vivid experience is graphically recorded.

THE ART PROGRAM

The teaching approach used should be in harmony with the background and the age of the children. In planning a program, the art teacher considers the needs of the class. The present skills shown by the children will, in part, determine the starting point for the program. The social backgrounds the children represent will govern the topics and the emphasis for particular projects.

Although children live in a world of global communications, it is still true that expression grows out of experience. Accordingly, their best work will be that which relates to the world they know and understand. They use art as a link to that world, whether it be real or imaginary.

There are three things to keep in mind in applying the environment-oriented art program at any given grade level. They are: an accurate assessment of the art skills and the experiences of the children; a reasonable expection of, and a plan for, progress from that point; flexibility in applying the program so that individual abilities and interests are developed.

Recognizing the diversity of abilities and interests among children of the same grade level in different areas and different school systems, we think it most productive to consider the program in broad terms. That means deliberately not pinning down a specific project to a specific grade level, but rather, indicating at what stage (early elementary, the middle grades, the early or junior high years) projects and ideas may be introduced most effectively.

Frequently, areas for art classes to explore will be suggested by other courses in the curriculum. For instance, units of study devoted to farming methods, transportation, protective coloration in nature, or Ancient Egypt would suggest a great many related projects for the art class. Remember, though, to preserve the integrity of the art program; it is not merely an appendage of the academic subjects. The arts are becoming more integrated with other subjects, but they remain as unique and vital areas of learning.

Children have drawn figures ice skating and then cut them out.

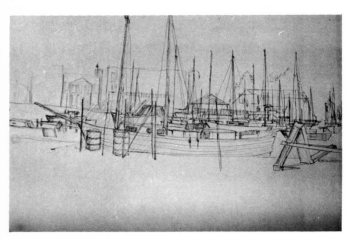
Making a careful sketch will sharpen awareness.

ART AND AWARENESS

The cornerstone for any effective art program is awareness. Since art is intended to sharpen perception, programs in awareness can be developed for any grade level. The students should be helped to see and understand their world and to appreciate its beauties. The first step is to encourage children to see—to *really* see—what they are looking at.

A creative way of seeing should constitute a continuing study, an ongoing discovery. It begins with the young child and focuses on simple qualities of the near and familiar—his classroom, perhaps. He is encouraged to see the colors and forms of the objects around him. Awareness of the immediate surroundings doesn't stop with those first discoveries, but increases and deepens. In the middle grades, for example, the attention may focus on the relationships between mass and void, on how things are (or can be) arranged in space. At this stage, the child may also observe shadows and changing colors under changing lights. Thus begins the conscious awareness of ephemeral effects, abstract patterns derived from surface appearances, relationship of light and shade, form, and space. Creative seeing—or vision—is a very important part of growing and developing. Hopefully, every art teacher will nurture this talent for seeing in each and every child.

An expressive drawing of forlorn buildings by a senior student.

In this painting, road and trees take on strong rhythmic forms.

17

ARTISTIC SKILLS

Learning in art is a continuous process as children grow in skills of perception and production. Particular skills are learned as the need becomes evident. Those skills help the child to interpret what he has seen and to translate his impressions of the world around him into creative statements of his own. Skill-building lessons are an essential and integrated part of any art education program. They are the necessary preludes to creative expression in which children learn techniques that will improve their visual communication.

A basic skill, of course, is drawing. And though the ability to produce accurate, "academic" type drawings is not particularly an aim of art today, the ability to draw reasonably well is.

A painting of goblets and a vase is under way.

Everyday objects can be interpreted in a variety of design exercises.

18

A still life in flowing, intricate lines.

Form is studied by means of a careful contour line.

Two onions provide an exercise in shading.

Perspective helps produce a three-dimensional image.

It goes along with learning to see—to observe accurately.

Composition, too, plays an important role. Essentially, it is the arrangement of lines, shapes and forms in an effective and pleasing way. It functions in paintings, posters, photographs, sculptures, interior designs—indeed, in all the visual arts. As they are introduced to the elements and possibilities of composition, children will respond to them and put them to work in their own productions.

Perspective is a very useful tool, and the basics can be introduced at the seventh or eighth grade level. If it is presented in conjunction with a sketching session, the principles can be demonstrated with ease. The approach should be imaginative, using subject matter familiar to the students. Looking at a street or road will show them that things look smaller and closer together as they recede into the distance. A little help back in the classroom and they will be able to create a convincing three-dimensional image on their paper. The idea of vanishing points and horizon line can be demonstrated on the chalkboard or "discovered" in student work. Students will see that exaggerated perspective can be a very dramatic and expressive element in drawings and paintings and also in posters, signs and film strips.

ART MEDIA AND MATERIALS

As successive years of schooling increase the child's verbal vocabulary, so the years of art classes should increase his vocabulary of media and materials. Pencils, crayons, and paints are the "basics" and they are useful from the very beginning onward. The child should also be introduced to the expressive possibilities of cut paper, papier-mâché, inks, wire and aluminum foil, clay and the many other modeling substances, plaster of Paris, wood, fabrics, film, and so on. The list of media available now for making pictures, sculptures, and displays is long and quite exciting. If the child has a working familiarity with a good number of the media, he will be able to express his creative ideas more effectively. He will be able to select from among many possibilities the medium that will best say what he wants to say.

In addition to working with the traditional media, a child will derive great pleasure and benefit from transforming cast-off everyday objects into his own creations. A cardboard box is a

The effect of corrugated cardboard is explored in this abstract design.

Mixed media (paint washed over crayon) gives a feeling of texture.

Cut and folded paper is used to make a puppet.

Figures made of paper can be stuffed.

potential miniature room or the chassis of a school bus. A tin can may be cut and fashioned into an animal body or an abstract sculpture. The possibilities are endless. The creative challenge for the child is in imagining the possibilities and in bringing about the transformation.

Variety in media and materials is stimulating and well worth pursuing in the art program. For example, young children should work often in opaque tempera paint with large brushes. They should also be able to combine other materials with the paint. Crayon can be used to draw a picture and then washes of paint can be applied that will be resisted by the wax crayon. Colored paper combined with paint or crayon allows greater exploration of material.

Printmaking opens new horizons for expression and may stand alone or be combined with other media. There are many techniques ranging from the simple potato print (easily introduced to the youngest children who will incorporate them into their

A pet portrait made from a box, cut paper, yarn, and beads.

paintings with ease) and crayon stencil to the more complex linoleum block or silkscreen.

Pictures need not remain flat. Some of the basic skills such as scoring and curling will be sufficient prerequisites for the use of paper sculpture in pictures. Pictures in three dimensions can be built within a box using paper, modeling clay, and papier-mâché. The children themselves will explore new dimensions and new media.

Children should be able to get whatever materials they need at the moment and should have free access to supply sources. Of course it will be necessary to have the occasional lesson where they learn how to use a particular medium. But with this basic knowledge of skills, they can then mix the media and stretch their imaginations within a single composition. As he explores new media and techniques, each child expands his artistic vocabulary, and he should use this new knowledge in the language of visual communication.

A sculpture using wood sticks is a study in spatial design.

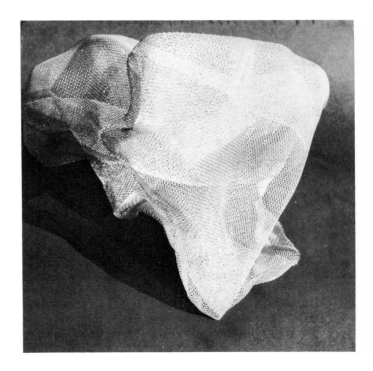

Light and shadow are important in this sculpture made of screen.

People are an important part of our daily environment.

2 Our World of People

Our environment is people. It is family, friends, neighbors, classmates, associates. It is people known and unknown, near and far. As each child grows up in the world of people, his awareness of his relationship to others broadens and deepens.

The most important people to the child are the members of his own family. The activities of the family are an expression of the society. As subjects for art, such activities are valid concerns of any artist or any student. And so, the home and family become the focus for many and varied activities in the art class. With younger children, it gives an opportunity to stress awareness, while older students will look for interpretive aspects.

Through the years, the circle of known people is always expanding. In school, the child comes in contact with classmates and teachers. He discovers friends. Later on, he becomes aware of the society of which he is a part. With maturity, he may even feel a kinship with people everywhere—the family of man. This growth of awareness and involvement with people will surely be reflected in his art.

Children's activities interest the young child.

THE FAMILY IN CLASSROOM ART

People are all around us. But, as has been said, the most important people to the child are the members of his own family. It is only natural that these people should appear in drawings from the time when children first begin to make representational pictures. Mother or father are liable to appear smaller than the child, partly because of a natural tendency to attach importance to size but also because the self-image has been made first and the others help to fill the remaining space on the page. These people in the family each have their own symbol to identify them; it is only in later stages of development that their individuality becomes distinguishable.

The younger child paints best when he is thinking of what he

A family gathering inspired this group portrait.

and his family have done. He shows activities around the home such as "Raking the Lawn" or "Washing the Dishes." His pictures go with the family "Visiting Grandmother" or "Shopping at the Supermarket." He becomes the focus of attention in such pictures as "At the Table" or "Going Camping." Pictures are media for communication and children have many experiences to communicate, most of them involving the family. The teacher will provide opportunities that will encourage these visual statements about home and family.

A direct extension of this early family-inspired picture-making may be introduced when the children are old enough to enjoy "team work." Use family activities as the inspiration for murals and other group projects. Children might work individually to paint large pictures of family members in everyday activities. They would then cut these out and work with the other members of the class to assemble them into a composition that spills over time and space. The assembling should be done by the children themselves, working in groups and with a minimum of direction. The group experience is an important aspect of democratic living—a learning outcome of the art class.

Children grow and mature, but their interest in home and family remains. Experiences within the family remain the inspiration for pictures. Use this natural interest to teach certain skills and abilities that are desirable. A subject such as "Around the Television Set" not only encourages children to show varied poses but affords an excellent opportunity to emphasize the overlapping that will strengthen composition. "A Ride in the Family Car" is one topic that uses a new point of view and one that presents the additional problem of an enclosed picture plane. Instead of showing the outside of the car with heads seen through the windows, suggest to children that they paint the subject as they would themselves see it from inside the car.

Each child's own family can become the focus for a special project in the later elementary grades. Armed with some skill in drawing heads and individual features, children will be ready to make family portraits and can work from memory or use photographs. (A discussion of portraiture per se will be found later in this chapter.) These portraits could be of individuals and then arranged to make a family tree. The teacher should encourage the children to use imagination in constructing the chart, per-

Symbols of a family were incorporated into a design made of fabric shapes sewn together.

After an introduction to heraldry, students designed their own family crests, painting them on paper fabric to make banners.

haps suggesting that some students mount the portraits on boxes or cylinders instead of on the usual flat support.

"Family identity" offers many other possibilities for art projects. Through the years, man has devised several ways to record his lineage and identity by family. On the Northwest Coast of America, the Indian tribes carved massive totem poles that made use of readily available trees to record the history of the group. In other cultures, heraldry was developed to identify clans. Today, we use the monogram or the family seal.

In the art class, children can develop visual statements following any one of these ideas to record their families. A study of heraldry and a catalog of heraldic symbols will suggest to them activities that are rooted in the past but are creatively contemporary. Not concerned with acceptance by recognized heraldic experts, children will incorporate into their designs the symbols that represent significant aspects of their own family life. They may combine several media to create crests and banners that are personal and communicative. From the totem pole will come interpretations of ancestors and family milestones. The creation of symbols for use in such totems will sharpen the powers of visual interpretation and abstract representation. Monograms or family trademarks will require some skills in lettering as well as call upon a knowledge of design principles and artistic skills.

Senior students, too, would be interested in such family-oriented projects as described above. They would bring to their work their increased technical skills, a greater interest in historical styles, more extensive research into their family histories, and a more sophisticated inventiveness in the forms they create. More demanding media might be selected too. Such designs would be very effective as wood carvings, ceramic plaques or silkscreen prints.

Senior students will also draw on the family as inspiration for pictures. This natural interest could be related to a study of art history. Reviewing several depictions of mother and child as evidenced in religious art over the centuries might be a prelude to work on a similar topic. Students could paint large pictures of mother and child in their own style or they might use the same topic as inspiration for sculpture, mosaic, or printmaking. Such an approach is a natural blending of the studio art program

This carved figure is based on a study of other cultural traditions.

The totem pole traced family history. This one is made of boxes stacked one on top of another.

29

A first grader's drawing of father, mother, and child.

and the historical context, a linking that is of real value in art education.

There are other possibilities for similar approaches. Many artists have treated the subject of husband and wife or of family. Studying several styles of a single topic will show students the variations in interpretation that is a result of the artists' personalities and social milieus. This will lead to a further investigation of cultural influence on the course of history. The studio work should reflect contemporary facts, but by studying cultural trends students will be able to understand better the influence of environment on their thinking. There is a place for such relevance of classroom and community.

A pencil drawing of a mother and baby.

Drawn from observation by a young child.

Crumpled tissue forces the child to make a very loose figure.

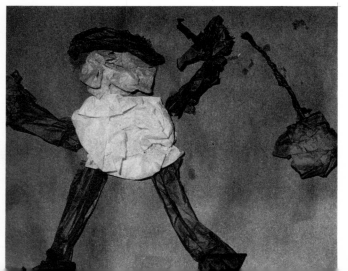

FIGURES AND FIGURE DRAWING

In beginning painting, children are likely to omit bodies from their people and to depict arms and legs growing directly out of the head. To help them improve the figures, have them feel their tummies, stretch their legs, and bend their arms. It is always helpful to imagine oneself doing the action to be shown in the picture. Stretching, bending, reaching, running, and twisting will help the children to feel the action so that they are then better able to show movement in the pictures. Making the person large will improve the picture composition. There will be no problem in adding a background if the figure is large and colorful.

With younger children, have them put the people in their picture first. They will have their own ideas and symbols for people, but will need encouragement to make large and active figures. These pictures should be colorful and bold, with children encouraged to make patterns and textures that add interest.

Soon children can benefit from activities in figure drawing using the posed model. Have members of the class take turns as models posing on a desk or in front of the class. Suggest that they bend and twist to make the body more interesting. Lead the children to see proportions and action lines. Have them draw the figures in light-colored paint or soft crayon. They should be encouraged to work quickly and freely. The children may use this framework to paint more detailed figures, perhaps changing them into entirely different characters. A bent figure could become an old man while another pose might suggest a skater or a dancer. Working quickly will help the students to show action and life in the figures. Large size requires big arm movements that are worthwhile at any age level.

There are many figure drawing exercises that will help children to gain skills. Painting on wet paper loosens the drawings. Working with solid areas of color rather than line shows the weight of the figure. Scrubbing paint from a dry brush makes the figures more textured. Tearing figures from lightweight paper will allow for only broad actions. Crayon lines could be added for details. Using the sides of broken pieces of crayon results in loose and lively drawings. Crayon resist techniques (in which the outline is drawn in thick wax crayon and then washed over with paint) allows the addition of details. Combinations of materials

Heavy foil has been shaped into dancing figures.

Paper dipped in paste was wrapped over a wire frame.

Paper pulp was plastered over a wire armature and then painted for this figure of a golfer.

Plaster strip draped over a paper and wire armature works well for figures.

Action should be emphasized in three-dimensional figures.

Children's figure drawings can be evocative and imaginative.

Drawings done from the model have a life and vitality.

will help children to realize the limitations and potential of each. Painting freely on printed newspapers suggests form and texture to the figures. Some older students may want to make more precise drawings using ink or felt-tip markers. Using a variety of materials and approaches will improve figure drawing at all age levels.

Figure drawing can become three-dimensional when students go beyond the flat pictures and explore different materials. Even boxes or scraps of wood will lead to imaginative figures when used by younger children. Paper and cardboard can be used to shape three-dimensional figures. Wire is useful in modeling figure-forms. Papier-mâché or modeling clay can also be used. Figures could be carved from soft wood or blocks of plaster. Encourage rather free forms that will be suited to the materials being used. Have the children note proportions and action in people before they construct their figures.

Figures should be incorporated into pictures and other art projects of the elementary classroom. Figures may appear alone or in groups but always will be related to the environment. Suggest that the children paint the people first in a picture and then relate the background to what the people are doing. Or have each child develop a group scene by painting individual figures so that they overlap and interact. The class may consider people in a group if the teacher draws attention to specific examples within the community. Encourage the children to note the actions of individuals as well as those actions that are common to the entire group. Have them use different colors and patterns to help separate the figures. In this way, the concept of contrast is introduced in picture compositions. Have children work in groups on large-scale pictures and murals. Encourage them to make the people tell the story of the picture through their actions and to keep the figures large. In senior classes, some students may choose to abstract the figures rather than use realistic forms.

For more senior students, placing a figure in the landscape presents particular problems in picture composition. Have them recall places where people are found, such as in a supermarket or on the roadside, and then consider the relationship of person to environment. Encourage them to look at people and study

A student depicts a group of classmates in action.

Contour drawings of groups of figures develop spatial concepts.

Moving close to the figure gives the student a chance to emphasize mood and detail.

A sweeping gesture gives this figure movement.

details of clothing. Have them think about the background and how it forms a setting for the picture. Then suggest that they attempt to show depth in the picture by bringing the figure into the foreground. Perhaps the person will be so close that he comes right out of the paper. It may be helpful to the student to find similar examples in magazine advertising and in professional paintings.

Torn paper is especially good for action figures.

Combining paint and printed paper helps to emphasize the action.

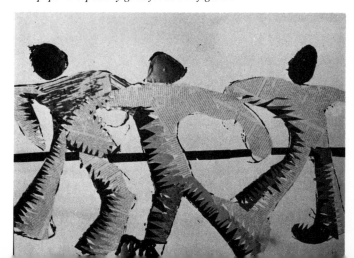

The teacher should look for unusual subject matter in which the student will have an opportunity to express original ideas. It is very important for the student to consider the character of the figure study and the effect of the chosen environment. Some members of the class may continue such a study to develop abstract compositions. Those interested in creating abstract sketches or paintings based on the figure would find a study of some of the Cubist paintings by Picasso very helpful.

Children's drawings have a simple directness of style.

Figures can be abstracted into imaginative designs.

Simplified figures of cut paper create an overall design.

Fun in the snow is captured in a textured painting.

These figures were shaped from colored tissue paper and then drawn over.

PORTRAITURE

Portraiture has a magnetic appeal for all ages. The face is an expressive summary of the whole person. To create a likeness of the face is, in a sense, to "capture" the person. In this, there is a sort of wonder and magic to which children respond enthusiastically.

In the elementary grades there is no reason for formal instruction on the anatomy of the face, but there is validity in an emphasis on facial characteristics from the early grades on. When young children want to draw a head, encourage them to touch their eyes, ears, nose, and mouth to realize that these features are important in their pictures.

The older students in the elementary school will welcome an opportunity to develop their portrait-making skills. First, give them a basic lesson in drawing heads. Using their own or their classmate's face, show them the basic divisions of the head. Do point out that not all faces fit a standard pattern but that it is possible to discover some general dimensions. The placement of eyes halfway down the head can be remembered if the extended fingers and thumb are used to show that the distance from eye to top of head is approximately equal to the distance from eye to chin. Introduce drawing media such as soft pencils, crayon, chalk, or charcoal, and have the children draw general heads so that they realize the need to show the underlying structure before attempting individual likenesses.

With some general knowledge of facial anatomy and as a result of the drawing exercises, students will be ready to attempt portraits of one another. The portraits should be lifesize or slightly smaller. They should be done in short sittings and will require a careful analysis of the individual features. The face is built on a basic framework which recognizes the relative placement of features. Have the children try several fairly quick sketches in which the aim is to capture the overall impression of head and features. If these sketches are lightly drawn, heavier, more carefully observed lines might be added to describe the features more emphatically.

The students can be urged to attempt self-portraits, using a hand mirror brought from home. Encourage honest effort and let the children realize that the problems in drawing a recogniz-

Individuality is evident in faces and figures.

able likeness are complex and not essential to successful pictures. It is best to draw the head just slightly smaller than lifesize.

An interesting project may be developed from portrait-making. Have the children make portraits of their family. They may draw or paint each member individually or create a group portrait in a single picture. In the group portrait, point out that the arrangement of the figures is important to the composition. Also, in the portraits, each member of the family should be distinguishable. Encourage children to bring photographs of the family that can be displayed alongside their drawings. The object is not to point up flaws in realism, but rather to stress to the children that people are individuals even though there are common traits within the family.

A simple, direct portrait head.

Using a posed model, the senior student creates a strong drawing.

Children can draw from the model, using one of their classmates or the teacher.

Portraiture by senior students requires a careful study of the face.

Faces are good subjects for block prints.

The student can capture the mood of a moment in a portrait.

An adjunct of portraiture is caricature, which is based on the exaggeration of an individual's form and features. Some students will be eager to try this humorous form of expression. Caricature is often used in illustrating magazine articles about famous people, and one way to learn the techniques of caricature would be to collect and study several of these examples. As with any such material, these are only sparks to individual and original efforts; they are never meant to be copied.

It is only senior students who will be likely to realize the role of portraiture in depicting personality. The elementary school art program should, however, work towards developing skills of perception that will make such understanding possible. We understand individuality better when we attempt to show it through portraiture.

The city street becomes an art environment with an exhibit of portraits.

A shape of colored paper is used for the mouth of this pastel figure.

Strong loose lines give this drawing an expressionistic quality.

CLOTHING, COSTUME AND FASHION DESIGN

The clothing people wear reveals much about them. Besides being a protective covering, clothing is a reflection of an individual's and a society's values and way of life. Clothing may express the extremes from individual idiosyncrasy to submerged individuality (one purpose of armed services uniforms). Clothing may be gaudy or plain, functional or wildly impractical. Most certainly it is always interesting in itself and in what it tells us of ourselves and others.

The youngest children are enchanted by costumes. A whole world of fantasy surrounds "dressing up." In his vivid imagination, the child becomes a cowboy, a pirate, a sailor, or a king. These dress-up experiences lend themselves beautifully to picture-making in the early elementary grades. The teacher might suggest that the children draw a Halloween costume they wore or saw. A discussion of some of the articles of clothing depicted will make the children more aware of the relation between the appearance of the costume and its function.

In the early years, children will draw and paint innumerable pictures of themselves and the people closest to them. The teacher can encourage them to observe or remember interesting things about the clothing to include in their pictures.

The study of fashion will appeal to many children and will suggest a variety of art projects. Fashion affects our environment, especially as more and more people tend to follow the lead of others in fashion. Looking at clothing worn to class will reveal many different styles as well as common trends. Have children paint new fashions on people in their pictures. Encourage them to use imagination in the fashions painted.

Colored paper and bits of fabric may be used to create a pictorial fashion show. Figures could be drawn in crayon or paint and then dressed in the other materials. Several children might work together to create a mural or frieze. Suggest that they do some research on fashion throughout history. Children will discover many books, pictures, and films that will help them. Encourage them to notice the fashions shown in paintings. These changing fashions may then be shown in pictures, murals, or

A child's painting of a group of skaters shows careful observation of the colorful clothing.

44

wall charts. They will be shown in a variety of materials with the children free to choose those that best suit their individual ideas. Some may want to make three-dimensional compositions working on wire, wood, or cardboard figure-forms they have made themselves. Crepe paper, colored tissue or paper fabric is good for these fashions, and designs can be applied using printmaking techniques.

Details of clothing can inspire interesting studies.

Paper sculpture showing an elaborate traditional Indian costume.

Each sports uniform is designed to meet the requirements of the particular game.

Looking for suitable fabric for the garment in such a cut-out picture as this enhances a child's awareness of costume design.

The real fun comes in making one's own original fashion creations. By draping cloth over one another, children will be able to create simple fashions. They need not know elaborate sewing skills to create costumes from inexpensive fabric. Paper fabric is also good because it can be glued instead of being sewn, if desired.

Fashion has been an important concern for many years. Students will enjoy even a casual exploration into the world of fashion. Have them talk to a local fashion designer or a tailor. Suggest that they make a montage of fashion illustrations from magazines or newspapers. Use overhead transparencies made by the students to show changing fashions. A group might create a classroom fashion show or develop a special puppet play in which costumes are featured.

Puppetry provides many opportunities to study costume.

Bits of fabric can be used expressively to create a picture.

Senior girls have designed and made their own fashions.

A fashion show in the classroom.

Appliqué design and a fringe are featured in this girl's skirt.

47

A PROJECT ON MASKS

The environment of an entire school was changed when children from all grades participated in an integrated project on masks. The week began with general presentations using films and slides to acquaint students with some of the uses of masks in various cultures. Further research materials were provided by the school library, and students were encouraged to report on individual experiences and research findings.

Different classes took different approaches to the study of mask cultures, often determined by the ages of the children and their previous experiences. They considered masks in several areas of studies as teachers integrated the special project with the regular school program. Ceremonial masks seemed to have special appeal and children learned about several tribal cultures that used masks. Theatrical masks were also considered as were those used for masquerades and festivals.

Students were then encouraged to form their own groups for projects leading to the "Ceremony of the Masks." These groups often ignored usual classroom divisions and frequently changed through the week. The groups chose different materials to make their own masks, each building a planned unit for presentation to the rest of the school. Some students made masks of papier-mâché either to wear or for decorations. Others made masks from natural materials, while certain groups painted banners on paper fabric. The teachers and student leaders met frequently to exchange ideas and to plan the final presentation.

The mask can be related to a study of native traditions.

Imaginative, masklike designs were painted on a paper banner.

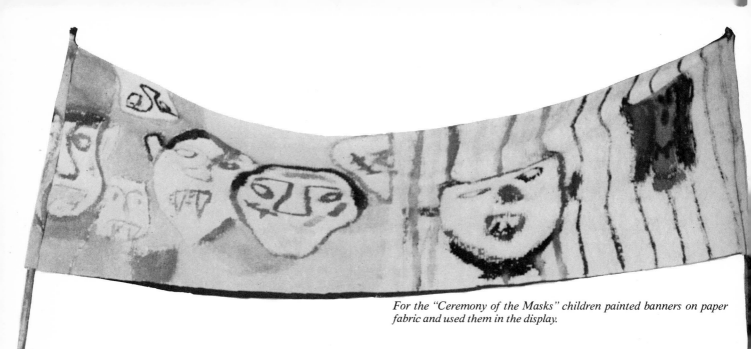

For the "Ceremony of the Masks" children painted banners on paper fabric and used them in the display.

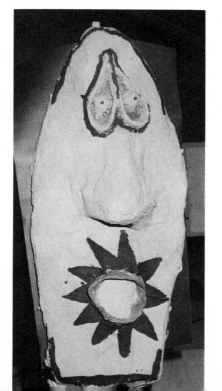

The culmination took the form of a display and stage production. Some illustrations in color may be seen on page 76. Students put their masks together into an auditorium exhibit, grouping them according to purpose or medium. They carefully planned patterns of movement and arranged display boards to direct the viewer through the exhibit. One group constructed a small room including masks, artifacts, and costumed figures to create an atmosphere of mystery. Another prepared a short pantomine using ceremonial masks and a witchcraft chant. A brief stage presentation included a historical review of masks using both actual objects and masks made by the students. The "Ceremony of the Masks" was staged in a continuous performance for other students in the school and for interested parents.

The large mask was made by modeling paper dipped in paste over a frame fashioned of chicken wire and wood.

One child created an imaginative masklike design.

Papier-mâché masks were grouped on the table for display.

A display points out the threat posed by the population explosion.

SOCIAL COMMENTARY

Many pictures made by children contain an element of social comment. Even young children unconsciously show their reactions to society by placing themselves in a large and central position within the picture. The secondary importance of parents and others has been echoed in the professional works of Marisol. The colors and patterns chosen by children may also be a visual communicating of reactions to environment.

Senior students will be much more explicit in their social commentary. Again, pictures are the most obvious form for such statements. In paintings of groups, students will show the importance of certain individuals, while others are pushed into the background. The choice of subject matter also indicates a personal outlook on society. War and misery appear often as a reaction against social ills. Dress and hair styles in the pictures, as well as the actions shown, often indicate an evaluation of their peers as well as of their elders. Young people are very perceptive, especially if they have enjoyed a strong program of art education.

Posters are particularly suited to social comment. Let students choose their own subjects and develop statements dealing with such issues as pollution, poverty, or peace. The effect of people on environment will provide countless ideas. Younger children may be concerned with clean streets or with having a park or a playground in which to play. Overpopulation and pollution problems will concern children in the senior grades. Whatever is their present concern, the teacher can encourage them to express it. Have them create original symbols and posters that combine illustration and lettering. These posters may be displayed about the school and in the community.

Murals, mobiles, designs, film, and other forms of expression can also be used by students for social comment. Be careful neither to impose adult attitudes nor restrict individuality. Students will use a variety of media and explore several techniques as they communicate their own beliefs. Topics such as love or hate always result in perceptive pictures at the senior grade levels.

All creative projects open up opportunities for discussion, and social commentary is a particularly provocative opportunity for dialogue. Even the opportunity to talk and to express personal ideals lends importance to the art class.

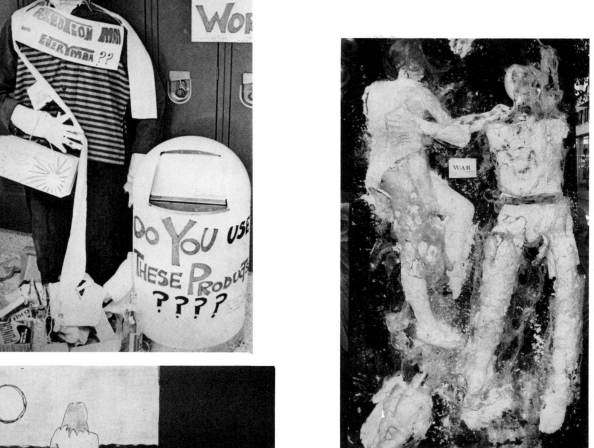

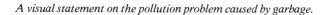
A visual statement on the pollution problem caused by garbage.

Plaster strip, plastic, wood, and found materials are combined in this statement on war.

A picture with a message focuses on the figure.

53

Children are subconsciously affected by the classroom environment.

3 Places for Living and Learning

Nearly all peoples on this earth construct shelters for themselves. Apparently we human beings need such dwellings. We need a place that is our own in which to rest, to gather with our family, to store our possessions, to "be." Inside and out, it is a part and a reflection of our immediate life. The shelters in which people live take many remarkable forms: palaces, huts, houses, apartments, igloos, junks, trailers. Whatever their size or design, they are "home." And home is the primary environment for each of us.

Men construct all sorts of buildings besides dwellings. They build structures in which to worship, to meet, to learn, to buy or exchange goods, to dine, to be entertained, to work. Each is meant to serve people in a special way at special times. And as each of these serves us, it too becomes our immediate environment.

For the young child, his home is his whole world, for that is where his life centers. When he is older, home remains important to him but he spends a number of hours each day in school. He becomes vitally aware of, and affected by, a new environment. These two places—home and school—offer endless possibilities for increased awareness and learning about environment from the earliest grades on.

A home of some sort is a necessity for every person.

In picture-making, the child describes his world. Children newly arrived at school will mostly depict themselves and their families. They also frequently include their own house. Drawing pictures of houses is natural even for younger children, and they have simple symbols to represent them. Often the home appears in pictures in equal importance to the people. As the young paint their houses, help them to recall some of the details such as number of windows and stories. Most will automatically show the television antenna even if they forget the door! This early training in observation and recall will be a worthwhile purpose for the art class.

As children develop, their early symbols for houses are replaced by more descriptive versions. As they look at each other's pictures, they will discover that houses are not all alike, that each child is showing a different house in his own way. Children can also recognize differences as they include the homes of neighbors in their pictures. Not only will they remember differences in houses, but they will also accept the variation in paintings by their own peer group. A picture of "The Houses on Our Street" will introduce the idea of rhythm to a picture. Although such concepts should never be belabored with children in the elementary grades, solving the problems now will make them more aware of their physical environment and give them skills to use in later work.

The design of houses is a suitable subject to introduce group projects. Have children each paint a picture of their own home, then cut it out and join the rest of the class in assembling a group mural. Although each child has worked individually on the orig-

The home and the sun share importance in the young child's picture.

Paper folded over cardboard makes a simple model home.

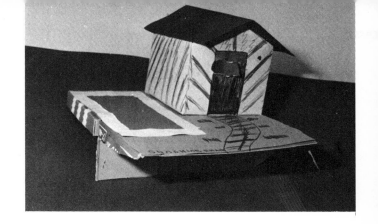

inal painting, he does become involved with the other members of the class in arranging the larger composition. To get the children really working together, have them paint pictures of their houses arranged along a long sheet of paper. Encourage them to add trees, lamp posts and other features, and to place the elements so as to overlap one another. This method of making a frieze is a valuable exercise in group dynamics.

There are many other ways that children in the early grades can use their own homes as inspiration for art projects. Boxes can be used to make model houses. These can then be arranged into communities, thus introducing the concepts of mapping and community planning.

Many children will become so interested in homes and shelters that this can become the basis for a study of other time periods. They will discover resource material showing homes in different parts of the world. Some of this will be in the form of slides and films they have seen, and they will recall the images from memory. Drawing on these experiences, children can create pictures, murals, and dioramas. The object of the art class is not so much to produce accurate illustrations of such houses as it is to help children expand their knowledge and sharpen their senses.

Making three-dimensional models is an effective way to show the home.

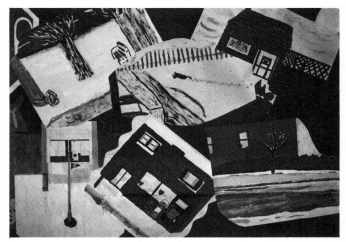

Paintings of homes by different children are cut and assembled on a background support.

The home is a favorite subject for picture-making.

A sensitive block print of a house by a senior student.

As older children examine closely the buildings in the neighborhood they will be anxious to learn more about architectural traditions. The history of shelter can be introduced as an incidental adjunct to regular art activities. Using slides and other research materials, students will research architecture as reflected in the homes of various societies. This will lead to a realization of the relation between architecture and climate and the effect of technical advances in the building trades. Art class activities thus become better related to the world environment.

By looking at their own homes and at the other houses and buildings around them, children in the elementary schools will discover many interesting fields of study. Whether it is simply a recognition of differences between houses or an approach to architectural design, whether a recording of interior and exterior views of their own home or a survey of housing styles throughout history, whatever is the particular emphasis of the study, children will find the homes that they know can be an exciting springboard to art activity.

One natural outgrowth of the early art experiences centered upon home and houses will be the planning of future homes. Even younger children will be glad to paint pictures of what their homes may be like in future years. They are likely to use bright colors but to adhere quite closely to present designs. There will be a few extra gimmicks and lots of decoration. Older children can be more reasoned in their approach, particularly if the exercise has been preceded by a study of architectural styles. Encourage them to explore new types of housing and free them of practical limitations such as money or building code restrictions. As well as making pictures of their dream homes—probably complete with a fair amout of detail drawing—children could build models using cardboard or styrofoam as the basis for three-dimensional construction. They would look for innovations in design but still emphasize the concept that "form follows function."

More advanced students will be interested in the architecture of homes and shelters too. They will be more perceptive about the similarities and differences in the houses they know best. They may have watched new houses being built and older buildings being demolished. Deeper awareness and a keener intellectual curiosity will be reflected in their pictures. Now they will

A model of a house complete with fenced yard and trees.

A detailed drawing of a mansion.

A knowledge of composition and perspective skills is developed.

Sketching out-of-doors increases the student's awareness of his surroundings.

Using dry transfer material, the senior student creates a positive and negative impression of à house.

Senior students can design and build model homes.

Historical buildings can also be modeled.

want to show details of construction and delve into the principles of architecture.

It is at this stage—at, say, the junior high level—that children should be taken outside and taught the skills of sketching. They may well have gone outside to draw and paint outdoor subjects in earlier years, but then the emphasis was on their own interpretations of what they saw. At this point, there should be some emphasis on the skills. Encourage the children to concentrate on one building and try to record what they see. Introduce a bit of perspective so they can see how it will help their drawings. Training the hand to draw what the eye sees is a long process, and can begin as soon as the child wants to record what he sees as he sees it. Further, by then his motor responses have developed to the point of refinement and control, his attention span is longer, and his patience is greater—all of which are important to the development of drawing skills.

These skills may be exercised in many directions. A series of sketches might illustrate in stages how a house is built from the foundation onward. A montage might be made of drawings of interesting houses in the community. A notebook might be com-

A study of homes of the past will give children new ideas for their art expressions.

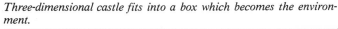
Three-dimensional castle fits into a box which becomes the environment.

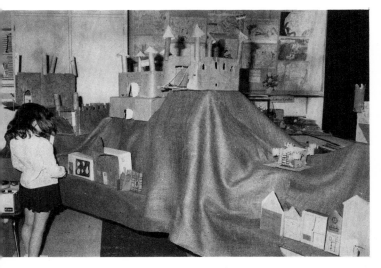

Small boxes provided the core of castles that were displayed on a table draped with burlap.

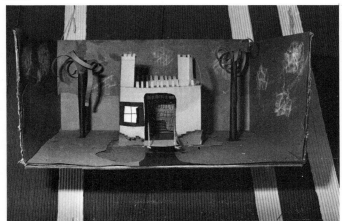

Cardboard castles cluster on the table.

piled of the elements of architecture or of many kinds of houses found around the world.

A visit to an architectural studio or even the examination of actual blueprints will arouse the interest of some students who have architectural inclinations. Not content with simple pictures of the houses they visualize, such students will want to produce detailed plans and projected renderings for houses out of their imaginations. Obviously, not all students in the class will be interested in such an activity. However, the art class is intended to be so structured that individuals will be able to choose those activities of particular interest. While some work out detailed plans and join in groups to produce precise scale models of proposed houses, the remainder of the class will proceed to other areas of art experience. In art education, students should be free to concentrate on particular interests or skills so long as they have a general foundation in the broad range of visual expression.

Boxes were used to build a fort.

Children have created an interesting classroom display.
(Photo by George Saleeba)

The works of students should always be on view in the classroom.

ROOMS AND THE CLASSROOM

The room is an enclosure of space. Whatever room we are in at the moment tends to control our actions—become a part of us. For many of us, much of our day is spent within the physical limits of a room. Children work in a classroom—the locale for the learning process—and even though the physical plant for learning is changing, children are still affected by this controlled environment.

The classroom, then, can be used to awaken in children an awareness of what a room—any room—is like—how it affects us, how well it functions, how it may be improved, what furnishings it contains, and so on. The child will realize that there is some measure of flexibility in the room or classroom environment. He will discover that the interior space is changed as furniture is moved about. He will realize that the whole effect of a room can be changed in countless ways. At every level of his development, the child can learn more about the room environment and its potential.

At the outset, everyone must be aware that the classroom is a special sort of room with a particular function. It is a place where learning is meant to occur, and it should contribute to good study habits. The arrangement of furniture and the decorations both should function for learning. The decorations should reflect the activities of the class and for the most part be the work of the children. They should be put up with restraint; clutter is distracting. In the early grades, the teacher will play a greater role in determining how much to display and where. Later on, the children themselves will be able to design effective display areas.

As noted in the introduction, awareness must be the first goal of the art program. The classroom itself is a good place to begin. Take children on an awareness trip. Move about the room with them. Point out the textures and patterns that can be found in this particular classroom. Have them touch the surfaces of walls, windows, tables, move around desks and tables to physically feel their shape and bulk. Young children will see the colors, forms and patterns that make up the classroom. They will record their discoveries through pictures and charts. Provide a variety of materials so that the children can choose freely. Some may work directly from observation but most children at this age will draw on memories and imagination to produce their pictures which should be worked large and boldly.

Younger children will not be conscious of environment per se and will not always realize the importance of classroom design. Yet they will react to their surroundings, and attention span and awareness will be conditioned by the atmosphere of the classroom. There need to be many visual stimuli, but as pointed out above, there should also be a restraint and order to the classroom decorations. Since it has been shown that children respond best to what they understand, the classroom should be decorated with work by children and well-designed teaching aids that are colorful and alive.

A classroom scene becomes an interesting art composition.

The disposition of the classroom is of great importance at every grade level. It continues to be an environment affecting learning and also a laboratory for the ongoing study of environment. Older children should also look at the classroom as a subject for pictures and designs. If they have been trained in observation skills in the younger grades, they will easily see the relationship of shapes and colors within the environment. Again, they may work from direct observation, perhaps cutting the shapes from colored paper and then adding details with other media. They might discover perspective and shadow from a study of the classroom. They may find shapes that are repeated or choose to work in three dimensions. Their awareness of the setting will strengthen the composition of pictures.

Beyond encouraging children to observe what elements make up the classroom, provide opportunities for them to experiment. Have them study the physical attributes of the room and then arrange and rearrange the furniture and displays. They will find that one kind of activity may suggest one sort of arrangement and another suggests a different one. They will discover the need for some kind of plan and order—that it is rather difficult to move about and function effectively if the furniture is placed willy-nilly, blocking walkways, doors, chalkboards and bookcases.

By changing the furniture around, children will discover function and efficiency. Aesthetics are involved too, for children will become aware that some arrangements are more pleasing than others. As they manipulate the objects and alter the space within a room, the children will appreciate the possibility of—and the need for—environmental control. Later on, this concept can be transferred to a larger sphere, urban planning for example. For now, each child realizes what constitutes a room (classroom) environment. He becomes more involved with this particular environment and more aware of himself when he physically seeks new solutions to the arrangement and decoration of the room.

The arrangement of furniture might be extended to creating designs for a more functional classroom area. Working with colored paper, the children can cut out shapes representing various furniture units and then arrange these on a large paper or board on which the boundaries of the classroom have been

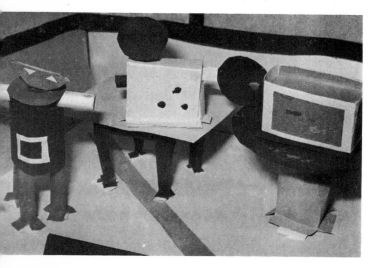

The teacher becomes a robot in this imaginary classroom model.

A cardboard box is used as the frame for a model room.

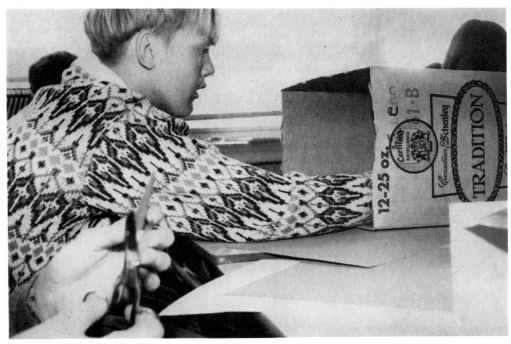

Making a model of any room gives an opportunity to try many design skills.

Furniture is made of colored paper, and the box contains the space in which the student may work.

The several displays in the room should be coordinated to give design unity throughout.

The whole classroom has been transformed into a great hall as the students study heraldry and knighthood.

drawn. The designs will be attractive in themselves and will also make the children more aware of the physical environment. Senior students might work to scale, thus integrating mathematical studies with the art experience.

Colored tissue and inks could be used to develop pictorial interpretations of the room. Some children may choose to make detailed drawings in ink, felt marker, crayon, or other suitable drawing media. The object should be to design areas with concern for the relationship of units. The transfer to an actual room will be quite easy, and children will also apply this method of planning to rooms other than the classroom. Although some senior students will welcome the opportunity to work in scale drawings and models, it will often be better to work freely and loosely, making an attractive and aesthetic visual presentation.

The room becomes a three-dimensional art project when children plan and construct dioramas. A box makes a suitable framework, and children will use paper sculpture, cut styrofoam, cardboard, or modeling clay to develop the furnishings and materials for the room. Encourage them to look for a variety of materials to use in these dioramas. Foil works for mirrors and coarse fabric becomes carpeting. The children will make the model rooms to fit their ideas. They will choose colors wisely according to their understanding of color theories. They might also use actual materials such as wood, fabric, or carpet samples to design rooms with an interest in texture as well as form. The amount of detail will depend on the age of the children, but even younger children will make elaborate models and learn about interior design as they work.

More senior students can plan room settings for specific purposes. These may be classrooms or living areas. Here, too, cardboard boxes or cartons can constitute the "shell." The students will begin by making sketches and plans. Fabric samples, color chips, and illustrations of furnishings might be collected at the planning stage. Each student will decide what sort of color scheme, style of furnishings, and decorating motif will best suit the room he is going to create. The students are then ready to develop their ideas three-dimensionally. They might work in groups with several groups later combining the individual model rooms into a house or a building. The object should be to create sophisticated room designs which will show each student's knowledge of art.

Attractive decorations welcome visitors to the classroom.

FURNISHINGS AND UTENSILS

In the preceding section we have thought in terms of the room or classroom as a whole. All of the furnishings were seen as a part of that whole environment. The relationship between the various pieces of furniture, displays, and other objects as well as their harmonious placement within the room constitute the total picture. However, individual pieces of furniture and the utensils we use are, of themselves, also good subjects for art class projects.

Classroom furnishings are important to the student. They are a convenience as well as an influence on work habits. Because children use furnishings daily, they will be able to evaluate the furnishings within their own classroom and also suggest new ideas of their own. They will design these as sketches or models. Some may even construct actual objects with the help of other teachers.

Encourage students to use their imaginations but help them to realize how form follows function. Large models of furniture could be built over cardboard cartons. Working with the industrial arts department, older students could design and build original pieces of actual furniture. In doing so, they will meet some of the principles of structure and construction. They see how furniture is designed to fit together and discover mechanical requirements of interlocking pieces.

Utensils that we use daily are designed objects that might well be studied by a class. Some will find it of interest to survey the history of particular objects such as bowls or spoons. They could prepare charts and visual records including three-dimensional replicas made from paper or clay. Such a study will help them in the studio program in such areas as ceramics. In this way, art history becomes integrated with other studies so that there is no artificial separation between understanding and technique. Making their own utensils is a challenge to students in the art class.

At whatever grade level utensils are studied and made, good design concepts should be stressed. The making of everyday objects helps children to recognize the role of design in daily living. They then become more selective as consumers and, hopefully, will raise the level of public taste in the long run.

Common utensils are rendered as a still life using a stippled technique.

WALLS AND DISPLAY AREAS

Walls are a part of a total room environment. Yet they, like furnishings, deserve a separate discussion. Walls offer endless possibilities for interesting treatment — both decorative and functional.

Children will be able to explore many of these possibilities in the classroom. Much of what they learn can be applied to rooms at home.

Art lends itself to attractive displays, but other disciplines need their chance too. The classroom should have the appearance of a working area for children. It should display what they are producing in various subjects as well as photographs, maps, and other materials that relate to the subjects being studied. Groupings of these visual materials should be attractively arranged on the walls and at a level and location where they can easily be seen by the children.

In some instances, wall areas may be used to paint on directly. Children of all ages have an affinity for leaving their "marks" on walls. Having a wall on which to paint will direct this urge into creative channels and at the same time teach volumes about design and also about the "integrity" of walls. Just seeing a wall that they have carefully and beautifully decorated will make many children aware of how really ugly and unpleasant are walls that have been thoughtlessly defaced with spray-paint, graffiti, or whatever.

To welcome visitors to a special display in their classroom, primary-school children constructed and decorated their own rose arbor.

A display should always be fitted to the room that holds it.

The young child paints what he sees in his world. This may be from actual experience or reflect information received from other sources.

As the child matures, he becomes more aware of the environment of his picture. Some fill the page completely, crowding the figures with color.

The school building becomes a gallery for student art work as in this example of colored designs placed over the windows.

Taking student art into the community is important.

If a classroom wall (or a portion thereof) is available, there is the question of what paint to use. Tempera colors mixed with polymer medium make inexpensive paints that will adhere to most wall surfaces. Or wall paint can be purchased in small quantities for use by the students. Acrylics are now available for classroom use.

The classroom wall belongs to everyone in the class, so decorating it with a mural should be a group project, with every child having a part. The children should first consider the wall as a design problem, being mindful of its essential quality of flatness and solidity. The design is then worked out on paper and tested for visual impact. That design might be a collage, consisting of details contributed by each child. When the overall design is satisfactory to everyone, it can be transferred to the wall using an overhead projector and then the artists are ready to go to work. Urge them to use strong colors and bold designs for best results. Senior students, with a better understanding of design principles, will create imaginative supergraphics. Younger children might work on paper, cardboard, or building board that has been fastened to the wall and can later be removed or painted over. Wall paintings such as this open new vistas to the students and show them the place of art in our interior environment.

The wall is a challenge to the artist. He has a wide variety of

A more formal arrangement of work is suited to a gallery setting.

Spacing is important to good display of work.

Abstract forms on a permanent mural done by students have been inspired by shapes in the environment.

Students have changed a whole wall to create an environment.

materials and techniques that can be used to improve its visual and tactile qualities. Many of these techniques may involve the making of tapestries or the working with fabric and yarn. Macramé and knitting techniques will appeal to many students and can be used in the classroom to create pleasing wall hangings. Burlap or other coarse fabric is an ideal support for projects in creative stitchery. Suggest that colored yarns or bits of fabric be used to develop the designs. Only simple stitches need be taught, since children will then invent their own ways of applying the yarn designs. Encourage a variety of materials within any one hanging. Have the class design several hangings, each with a particular display area in mind. Each child can work quite large, or several individuals can create smaller panels which are later combined into a group effort. In using burlap as a background support, children will soon discover that they can pull the threads, tie parts together, or otherwise change the fabric as well as adding new materials.

Finally, there may be a lack of wall surfaces. This offers the opportunity to explore how display surfaces may be contrived and space may be manipulated—spaces "created"—with movable room dividers, folding screens, large wall hangings suspended from the ceiling, and so on. Open concept areas present new challenges to teacher ingenuity since they do not have as much wall space for display. Some work may be suspended from the ceiling but this must be limited so as to avoid clutter. Portable display units are usually available or can be built from boxes or similar support surfaces. Again, involve the children in designing and mounting the displays, but offer the wisdom of experience and restraint.

Large-scale paintings are useful for decorating rooms.

Masks made in a variety of materials were the focal point for the "Ceremony of the Masks." A number of classes worked over an extended period in researching and preparing the production.

The mask is the special feature of a simple costume for one of the actors in the "Ceremony of the Masks."

Using masks they have created and other materials gathered from the environment, these students re-create the atmosphere of a room in which magic might be practised.

76

New techniques are tried out in displays that create an environment in an entire room.

An important segment of the display reflects the impact of media on the world of the young.

Students planned their own visual statement on the violence which has become a part of their environment.

One part of the environment display featured fashions.

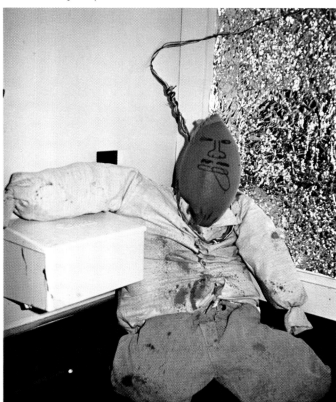

Traffic and movement are a vital part of the urban environment.

4   Communities Today and Tomorrow

As each one of us is part of a family, so each family is part of a larger community. Wherever we are, our community consists of those who live and work around us as well as being the physical environment for our life and work. A small town may be thought of as a community. A larger town may embrace several communities. A great city will contain many distinct communities within its borders. In New York City, for example, there are Greenwich Village, Harlem, Forest Hills, Jackson Heights, Chinatown, and Riverdale, to name a few. Each has its own distinct community identity and "belongs" to those who live there.

For a child, the extent of the community will depend upon his age. The very young child's community extends little beyond his home. Gradually, though, his experience takes in the block, and marvelous new vistas open on the wonderful day when he is able to cross the street. Even though he may have gone farther afield, as on trips with the family, the community he may explore and that he feels belongs to him is really rather small. Yet that community—his own neighborhood—contains a multitude of marvels and they are there awaiting discovery.

The child's understanding and awareness of the community grow as the child grows. Even within each child's experience there are likely to be several kinds of communities. Putting together many discoveries and experiences, the more senior student will see the relationship between the various physical elements of the community and, inseparable from those, the interrelation and interdependence of the people. He will become aware of broad patterns of community life. He may translate those patterns into imaginative and visionary plans for the communities of the future. Whatever the child's interests may be at each stage, his inquiring mind will be anxious to communicate his discoveries to others. So it is not surprising that the community should become the subject for many of the products of the art class.

A community planning project.

79

Individual paintings of buildings were assembled into a mural representing an imaginative view of the neighborhood.

EXPLORING THE NEIGHBORHOOD

The child newly arrived at school is exposed to a whole new world. The school itself is a new environment, often in a different neighborhood from the child's own immediate one. Take the children on awareness trips outside the classroom. Let them explore the rest of the school. Take them outside into the school yard to investigate the various play areas, the water fountains, the trees and shrubs, the fences and gates—everything that is there. Encourage them to record what they have seen in pictures and to talk about what is there—and why. Suggest that older children look for shapes that can be developed into designs.

The school yard and immediate neighborhood provide an ideal subject for a study in awareness. The children can discover and catalog the texture patterns in the surroundings. They can make rubbings of such surfaces as brick walls, tree bark, brass plaques, sidewalks, or manhole covers. This will heighten their sensitivity to the reality—the "feel"—of the things around them. The rubbings might be put together into a montage. Or they might be pasted onto cardboard backings, cut into interesting shapes and assembled into a three-dimensional object.

Even the young child will see much to draw in the community.

A sensitive rendering of a quiet, tree-lined residential block.

The postman is a familiar part of the neighborhood scene.

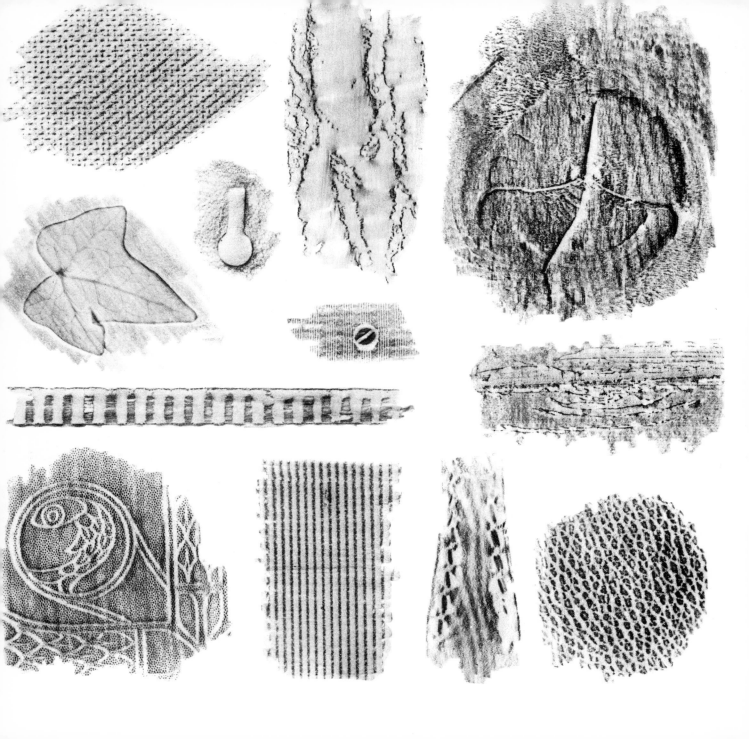

Awareness is looking at things that are often ignored. Suggest that the children go outside, choose a small area of the yard, and look for all the different shapes and objects in that area. They can make sketches and models of the area that will record the study. Some children will be interested in detailed scientific drawings while others will want to concentrate on shapes and textures as motifs for imaginative designs. The emphasis is on observation and interpretation based on a new awareness.

The view from a classroom window offers material for observation and creativity. Through the window—in which a small portion of the outside world is framed—the children can focus their attention and study the colors and the effects of changing light conditions. They may note many examples of overlapping—nearby structures, trees, or poles partially obscuring those farther away. The increased awareness of the shapes, colors, positions, lighting of the things they see will enrich their pictures and inspire their designs. Making a drawing or a painting of a scene from an imaginary window can make free use of their observations; the interplay of colors, lighting effects, and overlapping will be consciously used as compositional devices.

Looking down at a nearby corner.

Windows frame the outside scene.

A house from an unusual point of view.

Opposite. Rubbings of wood, leather, corrugated plastic, embossed book cover, molding, screw head, key hole, and screen.

The child in the earliest grades will describe the community as he knows it in his pictures. The kind of picture will depend on the age and experience of the child. Not only the technical skill, but the very subject matter, will reflect the individual. Young children interpret the simple environment they experience. They may portray the milkman in his truck or the postman, because these people are important to children. Dogs and other pets will take on an almost human appearance, and everything is likely to be placed in neat rows on a single ground line. Houses and trees will conform more closely to standard symbols than to visual reality.

The middle grades will have a far greater awareness of all that makes up a community. Their pictures may include a quite complete catalog of community buildings: houses, schools, churches, libraries, courthouses, stores, supermarkets, gas stations, movie theaters, bowling alleys. These might be cut out and pasted into a montage which will constitute a bird's eye view of the community.

Picture-making is not the only medium for recording the community milieu. Children should go beyond to other creative media such as silhouettes, prints, and three-dimensional models. Shapes discovered in the community can be cut from colored paper and assembled into an abstract design. Using colored tissue or acetate will encourage the children to make transparencies that are then used on the overhead projector. Older students could even work on a smaller scale to prepare 2″ x 2″ slides or filmstrips. Such exercises help to refine the student's understanding of design.

Pictures of the community provide many opportunities to develop skills and concepts that are basic to an understanding of visual composition. Studying an urban street will uncover a certain rhythm as demonstrated by utility poles, houses, and traffic. This rhythmic pattern will lead to other rhythms such as clothing patterns, queues, and blowing leaves. Some students might choose to capture this rhythm through photography instead of the usual painted picture.

The milkman makes his rounds even in wintry weather.

School is important in the life of a child, and here a painting has been made from observation of the building.

Opposite. Paint and cut-up newspapers were used to make this scene of a row of houses.

A modern roadway maze is translated into an artistic print.

The community is an expanded three-dimensional environment, so it follows that in itself it may be the inspiration for many sculptural projects. Plasticine and boxes are sufficient for imaginative sculptures. Older children will use wire and papier-mâché to sculpt figures and objects found in the community. Boxes can be used and covered with paper to make buildings for a model community. Sponges make effective trees in such a model, and children themselves will suggest other materials to use. Larger boxes will be suitable for model communities that are almost big enough to live in. Folded paper or cardboard is also a satisfactory medium for model-building.

Even with younger children no attempt should be made to re-create the actual community. Creativity and imagination enter into the individual models and the arrangement of the units into a composition. The community in the model created by older students may be a dream of future forms. A model by younger children may be greatly simplified by the limits of their skills and experiences.

The making of model communities might well be related to studies in history or to aesthetic concerns. Building models of past communities requires a study of both architecture and society. Older students will welcome the opportunity to create detailed models of buildings out of the past. They will arrange houses, stores, churches, and schools with consideration for community planning. In so doing, they also explore the realm of architectural design and will see examples of past styles among the details of neighborhood buildings. Models of future communities place the emphasis on sound planning and concern for the life-styles of people. Details added to model buildings will sharpen the students' powers of observation.

For younger children, the teacher can adapt those portions of the unit which seem suitable. Although these children will not be capable of a deep intellectual study of the community, they will respond to the stimulus and express their ideas in a wide range of statements. Working singly or in groups they will integrate art into other areas of study. Some may choose the visual method to report on their discoveries, while others will use verbal or written reporting. They will learn to look at the community, to see how streets and roads are planned, and how various segments of the community are arranged. Without realizing

Shapes found in the community are used as the basis for design.

Children have worked together to create a cut-paper image of a toy store.

A model of a community shows streets and buildings.

it they will discover the relationship between houses, stores, and parks. They may even suggest changes in the community, thus entering the realm of the town planner.

Talking to parents will acquaint children with the community of the past while they explore today's neighborhood. Learning to compare their own and other communities seen on family trips not only sharpens the perception but develops comparative concepts. There are many facets of town planning which can be learned even by younger children. More important is the concept of planning lessons in sequence. Leading children to explore in certain directions not only underlines the value of art but also sharpens intellectual powers.

In conjunction with studies of geography in the middle grades, children can produce pictorial maps of the neighborhood. Some may go on to recognize in the map a potential for imaginative designs. Resist techniques could be used to create decorative maps. Colored paper is a good medium, or shapes of tissue paper could be pasted into a design with the lines of the maplike design being added later using crayon, paint, ink or pastel. A three-dimensional map can be built out of layers of cardboard or styrofoam. In the art class, the emphasis is not so much on geographic accuracy as on aesthetic harmonies.

Within the community, the children know there are likely to be such specialized structures as churches, shopping centers and recreation areas. The development of their own communities may be recent enough for children to recall when such facilities were constructed and to realize the relationship between residential, industrial and commercial functions. They might use this as the basis for a pictorial map in which the different functions of the community are represented by different colors of paper. For the more senior students, it is but a short step from this to activities in creative town planning.

Pictures could also be made to indicate the growth of the community. Remind the children that there are many buildings in a relatively small area and thus encourage them to overlap the objects in their pictures. They should see that buildings frequently crowd one another and that some are closer together than others. There is ample opportunity to introduce many of the qualities of good picture composition as children record the urban environment.

All of the above may seem rather complex for the elementary grades. And yet it will be noted that there is some continuity and progression to the activities outlined. In the later grades, the older children will be able to explore the social as well as physical qualities of the community. It will not be every child who will be prepared to pursue studies in depth, but it is worthwhile in planning an art program to structure some obvious sequence into the lessons. The extent of the unit will depend on the age and interest of the children.

As they consider the community, whether it be through pictures, designs, models, or murals, students will become more aware of the relationship between art and life. They will discover many details of their own community. They will understand architecture as an expression of society. They will also appreciate the effect of environment on community life and individual activity. As they explore the community, children will discover the use of public art. They will look for ways to alter and improve the community. This concern for aesthetics in evaluating the environment must continue to be the major purpose of art education at any age level.

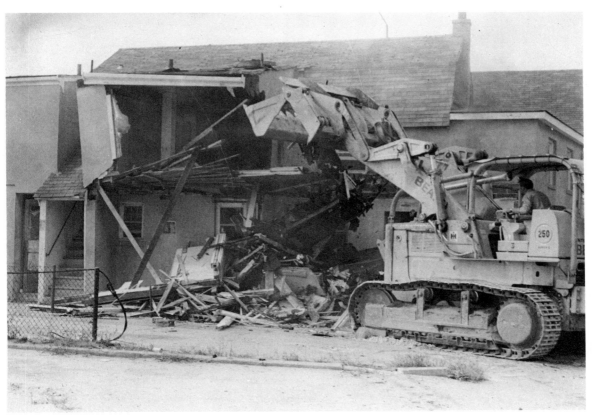

Children are aware that demolition and construction continually reshape their community. (Photo by George Saleeba)

A crane operator at work with his remarkable machine.

Expanding cities affect our way of life.

GROWTH OF THE CITIES

In the twentieth century, we are all inexorably caught up in the rapid growth of our urban areas. No matter where children live, they are aware of change and of ever-expanding cities. Few communities are lacking in some construction for long. Old buildings come down to make way for new. Neighborhoods change rapidly. All of this is reflected in the art of the classroom. Regardless of age level, children will find in the growth of the cities a diversity of inspiration for art activities. They will become more aware of their surroundings and be able to recognize different responsibilities within the community.

The city grows and changes. What will it become? Have groups of children work together to create models or murals that try to anticipate future aspects of the expanding city. Other groups might similarly deal with the city of the past. Have them record details of buildings that remain and note trends in modern architecture. But also lead them to see how a city grows and functions and how they can contribute to the preservation of a pleasant city life.

The inner city with its tall buildings, colorful stores, and busy traffic might suggest pictures, prints, or models. Children will also note changes in the core areas of cities. Generally, instead of growing out such areas grow up, as taller buildings replace those that are outmoded. Such changes can be a subject for model-building, and even paper sculpture will be suitable for simplified forms representing the towering city. Using different colors of paper and adding texture by cutting into the paper will improve the design qualities of this three-dimensional project. With such activities children will move from a rather realistic recording of the cityscape to a more imaginative treatment of urban concepts.

That cities constantly grow and change is dramatically illustrated by the demolition and rebuilding activities that go on day in and day out in every city. Children are intrigued by these activities, and they will realize that in them, people are actually molding their environment rather like a sculptor models clay. These activities hold many possibilities for art projects. Drawings or models may illustrate the sequence of construction and change — before, during, and after. Some children may be particularly interested in illustrating all of the equipment the construction

Cities suggest abstract shapes and designs.

The community becomes crowded and this is reflected in paintings.

Automobiles require a great deal of space. (Photo by George Saleeba)

91

City buildings are crowded together with little space between.

An unusual perspective describes the concrete and glass canyon of a city.

workers use—bulldozers, generators, cement mixers, acetylene torches, and so on. Others might want to interpret in a painting the hivelike activity of construction workers swarming over the skeletal framework of a structure.

Sometimes it may not be possible to take children to actual building sites. Here, as with other subjects, photographs can be used as both motivation and resource material. Films and slides will remind children of earlier experiences. Single-concept film loops are available as motivational aids and will introduce suitable topics. They should relate to the actual experiences enjoyed by the children. In this way, the photograph serves simply as a reminder and a spark to creativity. Photographs should always be used in preference to drawings or paintings done by others. Inevitably the artist will have inserted some individual interpretation into what he saw, and children, trying to emulate his style, will lose some of their own uniqueness.

Another aspect of the growing city that will be evident to most children is that of crowding. Remind them of their experiences in a crowded bus or a movie queue. To the small child a crowd takes on quite a different aspect that it does to an adult.

Masses of buildings are suggested by assemblages such as these.

There is much shoving and perhaps even some fear. There are many colors and much movement. The quality of the crowd will depend on the occasion.

Crowds are excitement, and as such are valuable incentives to art expression. Encourage the children to paint pictures of crowds from varying points of view. There are many ways to prod the child's memory and imagination. The teacher need only offer a suggestion. "Be part of the crowd pushing onto a bus and paint what you see." "Look at a crowd from across the street or from a second-story window." "Think of a crowd at a sports event and record its actions." "Imagine you are an ant or a worm and a crowd descends upon you." At any age level it is constructive for children to experiment with different aspects of a single topic. Older students might show their reaction to a crowd and its emotions through design rather than picture-making.

The senior student's painting shows a high-rise apartment towering over the surrounding houses.

The high-rise is commonplace in modern cities.

Work is under way on a model of a community.

TOWN PLANNING

Communities grow according to a plan, and town planning is currently a topic of some concern. We have planning boards and regulatory bodies, yet we complain about the destruction of the community. We see changes and experience different patterns of movement and qualities of life. Some of the concepts of town planning can be injected into the classroom art program. The extent of the study will depend on the age and interest of the children, as well as being influenced by the local environment.

A study of town planning might well form a unit of study to stretch over several weeks and to integrate with activities in other subject areas. Children might begin with a study of town planning in past cultures. They will research material from several sources and will be limited only by their curiosity and interests. Beginning the study with early man, they will recognize some of the attributes of community even among cave dwellers.

The cliff dwellings of the North American Indians are a source of fascination, and some students may be able to report on them from firsthand experiences on family travels. Others will need to rely on books, photographs, and films. Groups of children might work together to create models of the cliff dwellers' villages. Plaster strips modeled over cardboard boxes would be a suitable medium. Other members of the class could research and produce the designs and crafts typical of the Indian tribes. They could compare community concepts among the different tribes while recognizing some of the basic determinants of village location and layout.

The towns of medieval Europe reflect a different culture. Again, turning to available resource material, students will explore the physical plans of the towns and discuss the way of life at that time. They will be able to produce pictures, murals, and models that record the facts they have studied. Have a variety of materials available, and let children decide whether to work alone or in groups. They will discover the importance of the church or cathedral in such towns and become fascinated by the architectural glories of these great structures. Pictures and books will be sufficient to awaken in at least some children an interest in the art and sculpture of the cathedrals. Others will want to explore the art of stained glass. All of these specific interests can lead to classroom projects that will be selected on the basis of personal preference. Again, attention should be given to the evolution of the town and the mode of life.

From a study of the communities and towns of other times and other places would come a fruitful discussion of differences and similarities between those and the towns we know. Older children will realize that with the Industrial Revolution came the machines and factories so important in the towns of today. They will be able to discuss the impact of the invention of the automobile—and trains and planes. They may talk about the population "explosion" and the result in the crowding of cities and towns and in the shrinking of livable land resources. All of this increases awareness of what our towns are like now and invites speculation about what they will become.

Drawing of an apartment house of the future featuring irregularly stacked modules.

A design for a business complex.

95

An antipollution poster by a senior student.

The next logical step is to plan towns of the future. These projects should stretch the limits of the students' creative imaginations. At the same time, the plans, whether executed as drawings, paintings, or models, should take into account all that the students have learned about practical and aesthetic requirements. What a challenge to visualize possibilities for the future! Will our towns go underground? Will they float on lakes or oceans? Will they hover in the air? Will they be covered by gigantic domes? Visionary town planners are asking such questions now. The students might consider these possibilities and any others that occur to them. They will find such creative speculation fascinating and will develop designs for strange and wonderful futuristic towns. They may even come up with viable solutions to some of the problems presently facing architects and town planners.

A subtle poster speaks out against noise pollution.

Urban blight is a problem and a challenge.

Imagination leads to ideas of the future city.

Concerned with pollution problems, one student designed a domed city.

One way of travel replaced by the automobile.

Coaches and carriages, once common, are rarely seen now.

An ancient way of travel that is still widely used.

TRANSPORTATION

In one short century—which is no time at all, compared with the long history of mankind—people have totally revolutionized their way of getting about. For a million years, men have been moving from place to place on this earth, and in all that time they had but four ways to travel. They either walked, rode an animal, rode in an animal-drawn conveyance of some sort, or, if water was to be crossed, used a boat. Mostly, they walked.

Almost overnight, human life has been remarkably changed. We suddenly can travel in automobiles with considerable speed and no physical effort on our part. More astonishing, we can fly in jets that are unimpeded by gigantic mountain barriers, vast deserts, and oceans—jets that translate thousands of miles into but a few travel hours for us. So, whereas our forebears were restricted for the most part to a relatively small geographic area, our lives are characterized by wide mobility.

Young children will take automobiles, airplanes—even space travel—for granted, as though they had always existed. Children in the middle and upper grades will have a developing interest in the history of transportation and the startling transformation that is so recent. They will become increasingly aware of the effect of modern transportation on their lives. They may assess the drawbacks as well as the assets of cars and planes. They may consider all of the ramifications of travel that are challenges and, sometimes, sources of concern: traffic jams, parking lots, freeways, superhighways, airports, sonic booms, exhaust pollution, and all the rest. Transportation is certainly one of the foremost elements of our environment, and one that interests most children greatly. Their discoveries and studies can suggest many themes for creative art projects.

Young children will frequently include cars in their pictures. Soon, they will be depicting all sorts of vehicles: trucks, buses, motorcycles. By the middle grades, their awareness of transportation per se will have grown in many ways. They will realize that transportation is important in the expanding city. They will have perceived that automobiles, buses, subways and trains all demand their space to maneuver. And, related to this, they may note that bicycles, used by an increasing number of adults as well as children, have no such space accommodation. Perhaps streets should be designed to include bicycle paths. Children will be aware of attempts to improve the flow of traffic in their own and other cities. Letting imaginations take hold, they might illustrate their own ideas for transportation systems in tomorrow's cities. These visual statements could be but a prelude to group projects in building models, painting murals, preparing booklets or visual presentations on the overhead projector and on film.

Suburban living tends to be more spacious than the city, but here too the children will realize the importance of transportation systems. They will also note the grouping of houses around

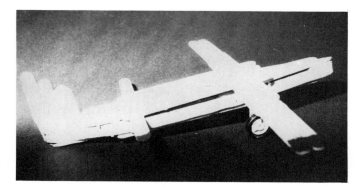

The airplane is familiar to all children.

Motor vehicles are taken for granted.

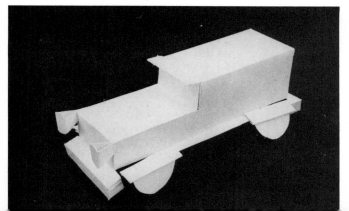

A display is devoted to the omnipresent automobile.

For some, "wheels" embody a life style.

schools and churches with ancillary shopping centers and parklands. The frieze or series picture might be a suitable technique for reporting on the concept of the suburb, but children should also explore other media of expression.

New roads bring large machinery and men with jackhammers. These are fascinating subjects for pictures or for murals in the elementary grades. Sometimes the children may concentrate on specific evidences of growth such as telephone linemen climbing

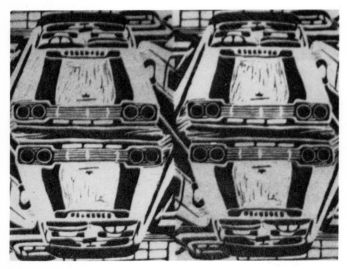

The automobile is used as a motif for printmaking by a senior student.

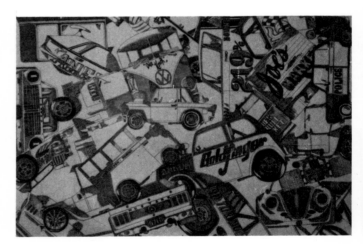

A welter of cars is transformed into a composition.

poles, workmen cutting trees, or bulldozers moving rocks. Have the children suggest several such subjects for pictures and then bind the finished work together into class booklets.

Roads have improved and towns today tend to be dominated by their streets. Children can show this through pictorial map designs or through models and sculptures. The highway interchanges of today are actually massive sculptures and lend themselves to interpretation in paper sculpture. Automobiles produce movement patterns which can be shown in linear design or mobiles.

Most children have been to the country. even if they have never lived there. They may recall the ribbon development along the highway, the pattern of the farms, the concentration of homes and stores at the crossroads that are typical of rural America. The influence of terrain on roads and settlements will also be evident to the students who will record the environment through pictorial maps, models and patterns. Many such activities will operate simultaneously in the classroom so that children can choose whichever suits them best. They will explore a variety of materials and utilize skills learned previously to develop comprehensive statements on possible future transportation systems. At the same time, they have some awareness of the way a city affects transportation and in turn is affected by it.

There are many ways to study traffic movement and the effect of roads on the environment.

A painting records one corner of an auto junk yard.

SOME PROJECT IDEAS

There are many opportunities in the school of today for an integrated learning experience based on art and the community environment. A few examples are outlined here as a springboard to specific plans that are adapted to the particular class.

In one school, students spent a week studying the area around the school. During part of each day, students were taken on tours of the area with specific destinations to allow them to study the environment. From the city schools, trips were made to such locations as unusual geological formations, area farms, and craftsmen's studios. On their return to the school, students were able to choose the media for reporting on what they had seen. Those who came to the art room were able to work in individual or group projects and to choose from several media available. Some depicted particular aspects of the study, while others took more of a general view of the area. In addition to creating artistic interpretations, the students arranged a display and made visual presentations to the class.

A project such as this encourages interdisciplinary study of the environment. Students learn the techniques of research and reporting. They are able to explore those aspects of particular personal interest. They can also choose the method of reporting that best suits their needs and talents. The school must provide many opportunities for learning and should help each student develop his unique talents and skills.

Another school also chose to make a study of the local environment but used a somewhat different approach. Students could choose a particular area of study in advance from a list of such concerns as technology, history, geology, population, or culture. Within each group there were several smaller topics so that students could spend most of the week in a particular study. One group chose to study costume. They researched the historical development of clothing and studied the ethnic background of people in the community. They prepared charts and small models to show changing styles in clothing. The girls then designed and made their own clothing, after a consideration of contemporary styles and a review of sewing skills. The culmination was a fashion show produced as part of a general performance reviewing all aspects of the study. One of the strengths of this particular project was the opportunity for individuals to make a concentrated study while still having a chance to explore several aspects of the environment.

Simultaneously in two schools, students were involved in an art and environment project that studied the neighborhood and included a variety of activities. In one, the several classes considered the buildings and activities of the older urban community that surrounded the school. The environment studied by one class was the school itself. Students were asked to look at the several classrooms and then consider the changes they would like in the school plant. This was an old school, but the students had many new ideas. They divided themselves into small groups and each started with a cardboard box that would be a room. Using paper sculpture they created the furniture and equipment needed in the particular classroom. A gymnasium and cafeteria were added, and in one classroom, the teacher was a robot. When completed, the box model rooms were stacked in an irregular structure representing the school.

Another class went out to study the buildings along the street that ran past the school. The students made large sketches of particular buildings and then used paint to add fresh colors. They were encouraged to paint with imagination and brilliance rather than being limited to the actual colors they had seen. The buildings were then cut out and assembled by the children into a mural. No attempt was made at realistic arrangement of actual buildings. Younger children used a variety of media to make pictures of school scenes. Most included themselves in the pictures, but the details were a good indication of their awareness of the surroundings. The pictures mixed materials according to the wishes of the individual children.

Another class worked on flat paper using oil pastels to color a picture of things that happen in the neighborhood. After the basics of the picture has been completed, the children cut and glued the paper so that it became three-dimensional. Other details were added using cut paper and found materials. Each picture required careful planning since the two-dimensional plane became the essential component of the folded picture.

The other school had one class involved in a long-term project on the environment. The object was to alter a vacant room so that it would depict a contemporary environment to the viewers. First, students used a cardboard box to create their own mini-environments. They drew at random a paper containing the name of something which would live or be found in their environment. Some of the things listed were: moth, pilot, fish, worm, hammer, and needle. Each student then created a suitable environment within the cardboard box, thus realizing the effect of point of view on the environment.

Other preliminary projects included memory sketches of specific areas in the school, paintings of neighborhood individuals, on-the-spot drawings of nearby buildings, and arrangements of signs that could be seen in the neighborhood.

The students themselves planned the room environment. The requirement was to interpret the contemporary scene, and they were allowed complete freedom within the vacant room available in the school. They decided to arrange portable display stands so as to channel the viewers through the room with displays grouped according to subject. The sectional statements included fashion, sports, pollution, war, music, art, radio, and television. Some of these are shown in the color illustrations on page 77. With a little help, the students divided themselves into groups for each section and developed their own visual statements. Because they worked close together, there was an easy continuity to the total display. The statements were personal and powerful. Other students, teachers and parents were conducted through the display and profited by the experience, but the major benefits were the signs of growth among individuals within the group. The students became more aware of the neighborhood environment and more appreciative of one another as individuals.

Students become involved in a local woodworking shop. (Photo by George Saleeba)

A student creates a mini-environment suited to a word he has been given.

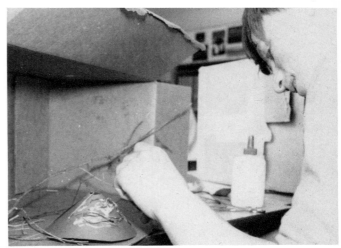

Outdoors, children collect natural materials to make rubbings.

5   The World of Nature

As the world becomes increasingly urbanized, nature seems to retreat accordingly. Technology has produced a quasi-artificial environment for nearly all of us in the span of a single lifetime, and that environment seems more "real" than the natural world beyond. Having never known a life directly dependent upon nature, children (and many adults, too) reasonably assume that life as they know it now is "natural," self-sustaining and independent.

This remarkable, man-made environment is closer to nature than is apparent. Technology—every machine, system, process—is totally dependent upon nature and natural resources. Nature is as necessary as the air we breathe. Encouraging a profound awareness in every child of this fact should be one of the aims of education.

Nowhere can an awareness and appreciation of the natural environment be given greater scope than in the art class. The overall art curriculum may be developed in three cumulative phases: (1) awareness and appreciation, (2) intellectual stimulation, (3) involvement.

The early elementary grades would begin with the discovery of nature—seeing the beauty and wonder in trees, animals, clouds, hills. The middle grades would take this awareness and appreciation further and at the same time intellectually begin to explore the mysteries of nature. Senior grades would add to the continuing cultivation of love and understanding of nature a direct involvement. Such action may take innumerable forms; all of them are aimed at preserving and restoring nature in one way or another. All are outward expressions by the student of his healthy respect for nature.

For this picture, the student observed the tree in nature and then added his own imagination.

Children become acquainted with a real wolf. The animal is tame enough to tour classrooms with his handler. (Photo by George Saleeba)

Prints made from natural materials sharpen awareness of texture.

TOWARD A LOVE OF NATURE

The beginning of a sound relationship between a child and the world of nature is with love. And love must begin with a closeness—a physical contact and trust. I recall the story of an inner-city child who visited a home in the country. She recoiled at the notion of going barefoot or tumbling on the soft grass, though her playmates did so with gusto. She shrank from the frogs and fish in the fish pond and seemed utterly uninterested in the birds and flowers and trees. The natural world was totally alien, and frightening to her. Little by little, though, her inquisitiveness and the example of others came to the fore. After several hours, the shoes and socks came off, and she ventured forth, wiggling her toes in the cool grass, touching and smelling everything. She tried to catch a frog, she climbed a tree, and she discovered that the lovely fragrant roses have thorns to be respected. She didn't go so far as to explore the woods beyond the yard, but in the yard itself, at least, for the first time in her eight years she was "close" to nature.

Whether a child has had little or much direct contact with nature, a teacher may safely assume there is room for increased awareness and sensitivity. Class excursions to nearby parks, botanical gardens, or woods can be fruitful, particularly if the teacher encourages the children to explore with care, noticing subtle shapes, colors, textures. Even the most modest display of nature—perhaps a tiny plot of earth with a single tree tucked in some corner of a big city—offers a laboratory for experience and a subject for wonder.

Younger children will often include animals, birds, and flowers in their pictures. Encourage them to make use of whatever they have observed—the shape of a particular tree, the "feel" of rabbit fur—and try to convey the special quality they remember. Suggest subjects that make use of natural settings. A poem read aloud will frequently evoke a sensitive response and imaginative pictorial interpretation.

The child who has a pet of any sort—whether dog, cat, hamster, or goldfish—has an excellent opportunity to observe and appreciate one of nature's creatures. Pets offer many subjects for picture-making and other art projects, and they offer as well opportunities for shared experiences and learning that will have

the sandhill Crane.

A poem read aloud in class inspired this second grader's drawing of the sandhill crane.

broader application to the natural world at large. Pets, even the most domesticated varieties, are creatures in their own right with their own unique characteristics and requirements. The range and depth such discussions can take are unlimited if the teacher provides knowledgable, imaginative guidance. From an understanding and appreciation of the animals called pets, it is but a short step to an appreciation of the many, varied, remarkable creatures of the wild.

Camping is rich in opportunities for picture-making and projects. A child's description of what he encountered or a story read aloud that is rich in descriptive details will evoke enthusiasm and vivid pictorial responses. Children's pictures may focus on campsite or on woods, stream, wild animals, and birds.

Such pictures could be assembled together into a montage or mounted on cardboard or on boxes to create a three-dimensional effect. In the course of such an activity, the teacher will have many opportunities to open thought-provoking discussions about the natural scene. What kind of creatures live there? What would a fire do to that environment? Are the trees and ground cover important? Such questions and dozens more provide children an opportunity to share their understanding and experiences. Even a child who has never been camping will gain some insights from such a project.

As children become more aware of their environment, they will begin to sense the pattern of the natural world. Instead of just drawing a seashell, students in the upper elementary grades

Sketching outside immerses the child in nature.

A tree bristling with branches.

Cut-paper trunk and tissue foliage constitute this tree.

Trees with fluid shapes were done in pastels and charcoal.

Surging growth is suggested in this loose painting.

and in junior high could be encouraged to find patterns in these natural forms as well as in leaves, ferns, and snowflakes. Some of these natural forms may inspire abstract designs.

Just as children should be encouraged to experience nature in many ways—through the eyes, and also through touch, smell, hearing—so, too, they should be encouraged to use many different art techniques to express their experiences. Even very young children can create the image of a leaf by pressing it on paint-soaked paper towels and then onto paper. In a leaf print the child will frequently be able to see the delicate veins and intricate pattern more clearly than on the leaf itself. Leaves and

In her drawing, a fifth grader suggests the alert character of her pet.

A senior student captures the sleek, streamlined quality of a cat.

After a visit to a farm, a child interprets the appearance—and odor—of a pig.

ferns used as stencils make lively silhouette patterns. The leaf is placed on paper and paint is applied with a sponge or spattered on with a toothbrush scrubbed over a small piece of window screen.

Some natural materials such as tree bark, dried and pressed leaves and flowers, feathers, attractive stones, or seashells can be used in making collages and assemblages. The objects can be arranged and glued to stiff cardboard or pressed into damp plaster. The point of all such lessons should be to appreciate natural beauty and to find uses for common materials in artistic objects.

More advanced students should be encouraged to continue to grow in their sensitivity to nature. Their observations should be more keen and varied as experience increases, and their drawings and paintings develop accordingly. At the junior high level, many students are ready to relate to the natural world in a more reflective way. They will respond to the subtle, "inner" pictures of haiku poetry and may enjoy interpreting them in illustrations. A growing empathic envolvement with nature will increase the student's sensitivity and prompt a greater expressiveness in his art work.

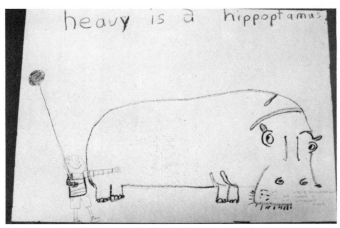

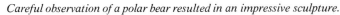

A hippopotamus seen at the zoo is described in line and word.

Careful observation of a polar bear resulted in an impressive sculpture.

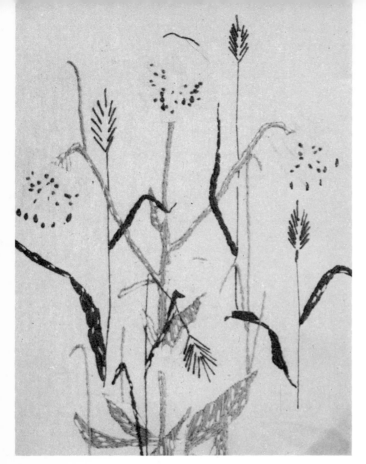

Weeds and grasses are the subject for creative stitchery.

A drawing of flowers around the base of a tree.

INTELLECTUAL CURIOSITY

Awareness of the natural world and a delight in its wonders is where a meaningful person-nature relationship begins. The relationship deepens as a child asks a thousand "whys," seeking to understand more about what he has encountered. As he grows, he may ask many of the same questions time and again, but with increasing maturity he is ready for increasingly complete and complex answers. These questions and answers can be explored by means of art projects at every level.

For example, a question such as "Where does the food we eat come from?" will prompt young children to think and learn about farms. They may interpret their understanding in drawings of fields and farm buildings, clay models of farm animals, and so on. Children in the middle grades will be interested in the diversity of farms and farming methods and in the effect of geography and climate on what can be grown. They will learn about the seasons and life cycles, animal husbandry, and the like. These explorations can be creatively expressed in pictures, charts, montages, murals, and models. Senior students will probe deeper into the mysteries and challenges of food production. They may weigh the merits of pesticides, forced crops, and organic gardening. They will be aware of the effects of pollution on immediate food production and the even more subtle and serious threat it poses to the delicately balanced food chain on which life on earth depends.

Because awareness is one of the most important objectives of contemporary art education programs, a variety of means of expanding that awareness should be explored. Children could concentrate on specific kinds of natural environment as subjects for art projects. Depending upon the location of the school, children could explore pond or tidal shore, swamp or forest. In these places, they would find many characteristic life forms and a multitude of patterns and textures. Back in the classroom, they could work in groups to create mini-environments that record their discoveries. Some specialization is possible in such a project, with different students being assigned such tasks as background painting, model building, frame construction, lettering, and assembling. Such projects that require group effort can be highly creative experiences for children as well as affording opportunities for constructive team work.

A raging forest fire was the subject of this sixth grader's charcoal drawing.

Several different kinds of imaginary flowers have been combined into an attractive display board.

Our consumer society clutters the landscape with cast-offs.
(Photo by George Saleeba)

INVOLVEMENT THROUGH ART

The love of nature and an ever-increasing awareness and under-standing can lead toward an active partnership between the students and nature. In such a partnership, the students seek ways to solve the many problems that a technologically advanced society poses to the natural environment. There are a great number of challenging areas in which this active involvement can take place, and many forms it may take as well.

Beginning with the earliest classroom activities, a kind of conservation should be a part of the routine. This is aimed at reducing the "conspicuous consumption" that characterizes our society now. Children should be urged to make the fullest pos-sible use of art materials, saving whatever can be used again, wasting nothing, recycling drawings into paintings, paintings into montages, and montages into murals. In later school years, they will learn why such responsibility is important, but the youngest of children should be encouraged to learn good habits. Senior students may want to research the problem of waste and its en-vironmental implications.

If the students probe deeply at all, they will find that the prob-lem relates very directly to the preservation of nature and to ecological balance. They will discover that there are two primary aspects to consider: the depletion of natural resources to feed the manufacturing processes and the business of disposing of the 360 million tons of solid wastes that result each year in the U.S. Translating this into more graphic terms, they will find that that means every person—man, woman, and child—contributes more than a ton and a half of waste to the environment each year. That totals enough garbage—soda cans, magazines, paper cups, broken toys, auto hulks, and the like—to bury a 4,700-square-mile area (about the size of Connecticut) a foot deep, or to create a mountain of garbage higher than a twenty-story building cover-ing the whole of New York's Manhattan Island. (A full discussion of this particular ecological challenge appeared in a special report by Gary Soucie in the January 1973 issue of *Audubon.*)

Armed with the facts and interested in the concerns of ecol-ogists, the students can become active participants in the battle to preserve nature. Their efforts, so far as the art program is concerned, will primarily focus on the use of art media and

Everyday objects threaten to swallow us up in a polluted world.

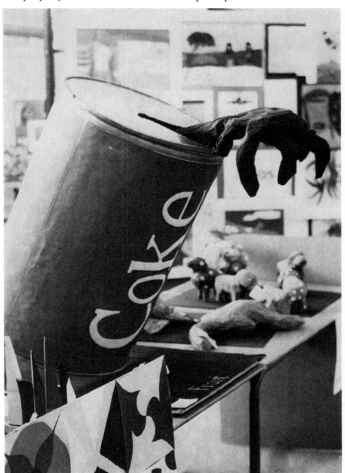

Seventh graders work together to clear an ecology trail.
(Photo by George Saleeba)

techniques. There are two immediate possibilities. First, having become aware of the problems, they will, through art, seek to make others aware by means of posters, displays, skits, television public-service "spot" messages, and so on. Second, they may seek to promote the solutions. This might mean working toward the establishment and use of recycling centers. For the science-oriented students, it might mean designing better recycling systems for the future.

The areas for ecological concern are many, and all can be explored by means of art projects. Some such projects serve to dramatize a statistic or a situation and thus give it a greater urgency and immediacy. Some may seek for practical solutions by means of visionary plans and systems. And some may demonstrate by means of direct action what is possible. Following through the waste and environment-depletion concern, this could mean collecting and sorting for recycling all of the waste generated in a given classroom in a month's or semester's time. Or a monumental "waste" sculpture could be constructed of the collection (excluding organic garbage such as apple cores and the like, which should be consigned to the nearest compost heap) that could be displayed. It probably won't be the most attractive sculpture in the world, but it will graphically illustrate what rampant consumerism adds up to, and the problems it poses.

Another example of direct action of a wholly different sort followed a study of the effect of pollution on the natural environment. A group of seventh graders cleaned up a section of woods and a stream and created an ecology trail. In regarding the restoration of a natural area as a creative act, they reflected something of the spirit of the avant-garde artists who devote themselves to "Earth Works." More immediately, they exercised their aesthetic sensitivity and their appreciation for nature by undertaking such a project.

To summarize, the natural environment, certainly indispensable to human life, is neither indestructible nor inexhaustible as we for so long have mistakenly thought. The need to rekindle a genuine regard and respect for nature, to be informed about nature, and to act responsibly toward nature is immediate and urgent. Through activities in the art class, the student can learn much in this direction.

A senior student has made a decorative ecology poster.

Students listen to a stage designer explain his model set.

6   Some Aspects of Communication

A bold poster communicates a familiar message.

Communication is a vast and complex subject. In this chapter, we will touch upon but a few of the aspects that directly relate to the classroom situation and the environment-oriented art program.

As a preface, we should note that learning is part and parcel of the communicating process. Impressions, thoughts, ideas flow back and forth between people, and as awareness and understanding grow, learning has taken place. Such communication takes many forms. We think of words as being foremost. Yet, much communication occurs quite apart from the verbal level. A symphony "speaks" without words. Without speaking at all, people communicate their attitudes and feelings by what has recently been described as "body language." Certainly, pictures of all kinds are powerful means of communication. It is important for children to be aware of the many and varied means of communication which inform them and which they can use to express their own thoughts and feelings.

Ours is a media-saturated environment. This is another facet of the broad subject of communication and one which deserves attention in the art class. Children may explore the commercial use of media and its impact on their own lives. They may study critically the omnipresent television set with its unending flow of graphic impressions, information, and entertainment. They may consider the proliferation of signs and billboards or the great array of newspapers, magazines, and "mailers." What function does each of these media serve? What toll does it take? All are a part of our environment; all affect it and each individual.

The modern media that surround us can be turned to creative use. Children can create their own signs, posters, newspapers, magazines, photographs, films, and so on. In doing so, they are expanding their own communicative means and exploring the potentials of such media for expressing their own thoughts and feelings. This active participation in the realm of the communication arts is an important part of any art program that centers upon the man-environment relationship.

Displays are a means of communication.

VERBAL AND VISUAL COMMUNICATION

The environment contains many media of communication and the child learns primarily through verbal and visual means—the same media he uses to respond to stimuli. Although art should be concerned first and foremost with visual communication, it often relies also on the verbal. Much of teaching is communicated through verbal channels, and the children often respond in the same way. Yet the art teacher should be able to utilize visual means to communicate ideas.

One approach would be to go with the children out into the community and look at the environment. Encourage them to look for the large pictures that encompass many buildings or much space, to seek out smaller details and specific areas of the surroundings, to discover patterns and design both in nature and in the man-made environment. Lead children to see not so much through verbal communication as through the *visual*.

Supplement the real and immediate environment with slides, pictures, films, and video images. Let the children add their own sound to what they see. Then encourage them to respond in visual form to the stimuli. The pictures they make, the rubbings they produce, or the designs they construct will truly communicate their reactions to the visual environment. Although children, especially the young, are anxious to describe what they have have done in words, lead them to realize that the visual is a powerful medium of communication by itself.

Often, slides or filmstrips can be used to motivate the class. Structure a sequence of slides that explores specific features of the environment, using images such as people, trees, water, movement, textures, or materials. Arrange the slides so that the particular feature is interpreted through both general and specific images. Do not try to show too much at a time, since the reaction of the children will be even more important than the original viewing. Encourage them to discuss what they see but lead them to concentrate on the particular quality of environment being shown. Then let them choose their own media with which to respond.

After viewing slides or filmstrips, some children may go to paint or chalk to make a pictorial interpretation. The subject of each picture will indicate the personality of the young artist as well as his visual acuity. Others will want to write or speak about what they have seen. Introduce dramatic concepts and show the relationship between movement and speech. Some children may even concentrate on movement as a form of expression and could go on to make simple costumes and to construct tableaus. Among other media of communication might be puppets, signs, songs, poems, models, and complete environments.

Out of the visual communication used as a stimulus (in this instance the slides or filmstrips) will come a wide variety of responses in which the children are able to draw on accumulated knowledge and skills to communicate to others their personal reaction to the environment. The ideal is to afford children an opportunity to respond in media similar to those used as stimulus, so that they will themselves make slides, filmstrips, and films.

Paintings, such as this one titled "The Lonely Street," communicate without words.

Advertising is everywhere and sometimes overdone.

A collage of advertisements gives the idea of saturation.

THE MEDIA

In the contemporary world, children are surrounded by media of communication. They are affected by what they see and hear so that these become an integral part of their environment. Children react to their environment in the art they produce, and so the communications media become a part of education through art.

The teacher can plan a number of activities for the art class that will capitalize on this familiarity with media. However, these activities should be more than a simple outgrowth of communication. Children should realize the impact of the media on them. They should understand something of the work of the advertising man. They should appreciate critically the media and their expression and importance in the world of today.

The child in the elementary school has available to him a wide variety of media for his own artistic expression and a sharp awareness of the media that are part of his environment. Ever expanding, the choice of media to interpret the environment is extensive and challenging. However, at this level, we must use media only as a means to train the visual awareness of children and to help them better appreciate their surroundings. Both through using the media themselves and discovering how they have been used by others, children will come to realize the importance of art in the environment.

Letters and signs in the environment can be used for designs.

ADVERTISING ART

No matter where they go, children are confronted by the art of the advertiser. The newspapers and magazines, the television, and even the physical environment are saturated with advertising. Because much of this is visual communication, an exploration of the world of advertising is suited to the art program.

Children might concentrate on one specific form of advertising at a time so that they become aware of the variety of techniques used. They can complete research projects and make collections of actual samples while applying their art skills to work of their own. They can discover the role of advertising while at the same time becoming more aware of their environment.

One form that lends itself particularly well to art class study is advertising art in newspapers and magazines. Because children have extensive exposure to this form, they can appreciate the visual style of such advertising and will soon learn to classify advertising according to technique. Making a collection of many such advertisements will allow a variety of projects in the art class.

Simply studying the lettering styles and illustrative approaches

Lettering should be chosen to fit with the illustrations in advertisement collages.

Students can choose a word and then design letters that will express the word's meaning.

Making a montage of magazine advertisements can lead to posters.

Collecting examples of lettering will make children aware of the number of styles in contemporary graphics.

Quite simple cut-paper letters can be used in effective posters.

Making a montage of magazine advertisements can lead to posters.

Collecting examples of lettering will make children aware of the number of styles in contemporary graphics.

Students can choose a word and then design letters that will express the word's meaning.

Quite simple cut-paper letters can be used in effective posters.

of such advertising will suggest the making of charts or murals. Montages of advertising can use complete layouts or smaller segments. As well as noting the techniques of the advertising artist, the students are able to apply their own compositional skills to the making of the design. A greater awareness of the print environment must inevitably result from such activities. Some may choose to concentrate on lettering and to build their montage out of words and symbols. Others will look for illustrations, perhaps supplementing what they find with drawings of their own.

Children can also create their own advertisements. The extent of the project will, of course, depend on the age and ability of the children. They will be able to create advertisements which may be used as display or may even be reproduced in school newspapers and publications. To create such work successfully, the children must first have some knowledge of lettering and illustrative techniques. Their picture-making program will have provided some background skills in composition that will make the layout of the advertisements more effective. The illustrations should be typically childlike and, therefore, will draw heavily on the natural and acquired pictorial skills of the children. Their examination of actual examples from newspapers and magazines may suggest extra ideas but must not be allowed to interfere with the freshness of youthful drawings.

Closely allied with newspaper advertising is the whole exciting world of the poster and billboard. Children can make use of skills in lettering, illustration and composition to create posters for advertising school functions. Because environment has such an effect on children, teachers should select carefully the work put on view in the classrooms and school corridors. Choosing posters that are well designed will help improve the visual output of the children. They should make posters that are excitingly childlike but that obey the basic rules of poster-making. They can use cut paper and other suitable materials and they should strive for individuality in the poster design.

Some children may choose to work on a much larger scale than poster size, thus creating their own billboards, neon signs, bus advertising, and other public graphics. Encourage them to be critical and to search out new ways to combine the world of commerce with natural beauty.

Younger children can cut letters from colored paper using the width of the strip of paper as the height of the letters.

Senior students will develop their own lettering styles.

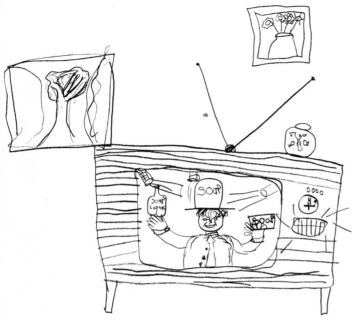

A television commercial is recalled in this drawing.

A detail of a display devoted to the importance of modern communications.

TELEVISION COMMERCIALS

Because much time is spent watching television, this may be a good place to begin a study of advertising art in the early grades. Children will be able to recall many commercials that they have seen and a simple listing of those remembered will indicate something of the strength of various advertising techniques. Children could discuss the visual images of television advertising and list some of the many techniques used. Although it may be difficult to produce actual ads, even younger children will enjoy a chance to draw their own commercials. The extent of the activity will depend on the age and ability of the children.

Have even younger children draw what they remember of favorite television commercials. They will add their own freshness to the graphics of the designer and will recall favorite characters as well as specific situations. Some of the animated commercials may well have the greatest appeal, but even these will take on new life in the hands of young children. They might work on individual pictures that "freeze" one particular moment in the commercial. Or they could individually prepare a series of pictures which are then bound into a book, arranged as a frieze or joined into an oversized filmclip. Suggest to the children the need for continuity, clarity, and maximum impact in what they do.

Older students may even be able to produce their own television commercials, perhaps advertising a school event. In many schools there are facilities for TV production and taping so that children could see their work actually being broadcast. The commercials might take the form of short dramatic productions with the students producing their own scripts, props, costumes, and settings. Or they may be animated features made using a stop-action camera or a series of pictures flipped quickly in front of the camera. The art class must be aware of contemporary media of expression and the production of television commercials will give the children far greater understanding of this vehicle of communication. The excitement of seeing their work on the screen will catch the interest of even the most unenthusiastic student.

PACKAGE DESIGN

The influence of packaging on our way of life cannot be over-estimated. At every level children can be interested in the variety, inventiveness, and ingenuity of the ways things are packaged. They will recognize that there are many reasons for all this packaging: to preserve the freshness of foods, to protect fragile objects, to deter shoplifters. They will see, too, that nearly all packages are also designed to sell the product within. The importance of package design as a means of advertising should be explored in the art class. Whether it is the young child setting up a classroom store, the older student exploring the design of boxes and cans, or the senior student inventing new forms of packaging, package design will take a variety of approaches in the classroom.

Many lessons can be learned from a classroom store, and it will provide an ideal theme for integrated learning in the primary room. Children could go as a group to visit a neighborhood store and notice particularly the rows of products on the shelves. Upon returning to the classroom they will make pictures that will show the packages and displays that impressed them. Although somewhat incidental to the main subject of the picture, such designs will indicate the observation of the children. Some may use the names and designs to enrich the picture while others will take an even more abstract approach to the subject.

Setting up a store within the classroom will give children an opportunity to practice design concepts as they arrange boxes or cans in rows and displays. Using actual objects they subconsciously arrange the materials in a design experience. This is not unlike the activity of the more senior student in a merchandising class. The art students will have noticed the displays in the stores they visited, but the actual arrangement in the classroom will have the stamp of uniqueness that marks the artistic background of the students.

Not only will children arrange packages into attractive displays but they will add their own signs and posters that permit further application of the skills mentioned above. Thus, the making of a classroom store encourages the integration of many art skills while also pointing out the relationship of art to other subjects.

Older students will be able to create their own unique package designs. They will first explore actual packages both as to shape

Everyday objects become the motifs for designs that might be applied to packages.

Two packages with effective simplified designs.

and exterior design features. Then they can create their own packages for existing or imagined products. They should consider shape as it fits the function of the box. Both the needs of the product to be packaged and the limits of shipping and storage will affect the shape of the individual package. However, children need not be limited to forms of actual packages since they enjoy more freedom than the commercial designer.

The box should first be sketched and planned on flat paper and then transferred to cardboard which can be folded into an actual package. Finally, the graphic design of the package should be an integral part of the package. Working on a surface that has many planes will be a new experience for students. They will try to make their design both fit the surface and identify the product. Packages made by students will draw on their knowledge of design, illustration, and lettering. They should be displayed attractively as objects of art.

Pop Art draws on package design for many of its subjects. After a study of this style of art, students can use the packages they know as subjects for Pop Art pictures. Even better, they can develop their own bold designs which will emphasize commonplace objects as subjects for art expression.

Package design exercises can be applied also to book jackets and record covers.

PHOTOGRAPHY

Photography has taken its place as an art form and is finding its way into the elementary art class. Its use as a recorder of the environment is fairly obvious, although the potential for creative photography extends far beyond the commonplace. Certainly, photography is a powerful means of communication. This being so, it is not surprising to find it used extensively in advertising. In a non-commercial form, the power of photographs to communicate has been developed into photojournalism. Here, a number of photographs are selected and assembled to tell a story or report a news event. Sometimes, just a single photograph tells more than hundreds of words.

In the hands of a child, the camera can be an extension of the eye and can help him to sharpen his perception and increase his awareness. Photography has many applications in the elementary classroom and should be used as an extension of the visual process.

Even without a camera, children might approach the art of photography and explore its creative potentials. Collecting a number of photographs from magazines, they can then use these to create montages or collages that show the camera as a reporter or a recorder of the environment. These designs should center on a particular theme as chosen by the children and should demonstrate the child's knowledge of composition.

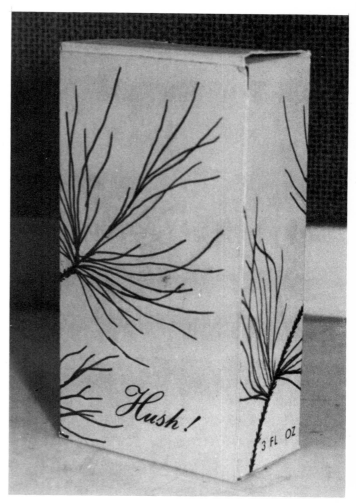

The students can make their own boxes from cardboard or cover existing forms.

As the children study the assembled photographs, they will realize that the camera has many moods and that photographs explore a single theme in a variety of ways. They will find, too, that the camera image can also be changed by fragmenting the photograph. They will discover their own way to cut a photograph clipped from a magazine so as to add a new dimension to that created by the camera. Combining two similar pictures to create a new image or transferring the photograph to a three-dimensional form are only two ways that the children will be able to alter the photograph. These exercises will help children to realize the creative potential of the camera and to expand their own visual vacabulary.

Many children already have their own cameras and will be only too anxious to bring them to school. Since many of them will have only limited adjustments, most of the photography must

Using a camera can help children become aware of interesting forms they might otherwise have overlooked.

132

be done outdoors. However, this will relate well to a program concerned with the environment.

Encourage the children to regard and use their cameras as an art medium rather than simply a mechanical device. Help them to understand how the aperture and time settings affect the exposures, and encourage them to check these settings before taking each shot. Also, discuss with them the creative planning and selectivity that goes into a good photograph. Have them each make a viewfinder by cutting a rectangular hole in a sheet of cardboard. Holding this at arm's length will help the child to compose his picture even before the camera is used.

The ideal camera for children is the Polaroid because it permits instant developing of the photo and allows the child to learn immediately from the photos he has made. The Polaroid camera is easily handled and can be conveniently carried for outside projects.

When the children are out looking for things to photograph they should be encouraged to concentrate on details of the environment as well as on the overall scene. Suggest that they note especially the effect of light and shade and pay particular attention to texture and pattern. Have different children explore the many aspects within a limited area so that they may better appreciate the variety in our environment. They will become increasingly aware of that marvelous variety as they use the camera as an extension of the eye.

As well as photographs of the natural environment, have children create their own subjects either by using their classmates or objects gathered and assembled into new arrangements. They can learn to pose other people so that the picture acquires a strong composition. The placement of the people, the costumes and background are all important to the finished photograph and are art experiences for the children. Similarly, arranging found objects into a composition and then taking photographs from several angles has double validity as an art experience. The children will look for details and textures as well as for form and volume.

Many of the photographs made by children will be done outside of regular class time. This is fine, for the subject matter can be expanded, and their photographs will reflect their own individual outside interests and experiences.

Developing of the film can be done through regular commercial channels or often it may be possible to have film developed in the audiovisual department of the school or school system. Some of the older students may pursue photography with great seriousness. They may have their own darkrooms at home where they do their own developing and printing, and they might be willing to tell about this aspect of their hobby. The developing and printing aspect of the photographic process offers great scope for creativity. The children will be interested in hearing about the possibilities and in seeing some of the more experimental examples of printing. Invite professional photographers to visit classroom and discuss samples of their work.

Have children prepare displays of the photographs they have made and try to get some of the better pictures enlarged. Much of the value in photography as a learning experience is really only obtained over an extended time period as children are able to learn from their earlier efforts. Photography opens new vistas for children and should be as creative an experience as other activities in the art class.

FILM MAKING

Among contemporary art media, film is one of the most popular and surely one with great potential for creative expression. Although at first it may seem too expensive for classroom use, the work on film by even young children opens new avenues for expression and can be within the budget limitations of our schools.

As with most other activities, the teacher should plan a series of lessons that will provide necessary skills for the final product. It is now possible to make colorful and imaginative films even without the use of a camera, but even here, some preliminary experiences with the projected image can lead to better use of the medium.

Children might start by making transparencies for the overhead projector. The large size of the working surface will be more in keeping with their picture-making in other media. Working on acetate, they can draw with felt markers or colored inks. The subject matter and detail will reflect the environment and abilities of the children, but the projection of the image will evoke new responses. Colored tissue paper shapes can be adhered to the acetate using polymer medium or a tissue glue. A second sheet of acetate over the top to make a sandwich effect will further protect the design. Inks can be used to draw over the tissue design. Children themselves will discover many other materials such as perforated paper that can be added to the design. They will need ready access to the overhead projector to test their work as a transparency. The overhead allows a wide range of approaches the design and permits the child to work on a fairly large scale.

The projected slide can also be created without using a camera and is capable of producing lively images. Again, colored inks or felt markers are useful on acetate which has been cut to size for mounting as a slide. Older children might experiment with other materials to create images on the slide. A fluid material such as mineral oil to which have been added colored dyes or solid objects can be sandwiched between two pieces of acetate and will create movement as the slide is heated in the projector. Unexposed film can be scratched or treated with bleaches and other chemicals to create patterns. Unwanted slides can be drawn on or otherwise altered so that the original image is ex-

Everyone can participate in designing and constructing the sets for a film.

panded. Cardboard or glass slide mounts are available at low cost so that the child's creation can be made ready for projection. Working on the smaller surface of the slide is a good preparation for later work on film.

Film making without a camera offers many possibilities for the imaginative child. Clear or frosted film leader is available at reasonable cost, and often films arriving in the audiovisual department have a long leader that can be removed and used for film making exercises.

At first it may be best simply to use colored inks or markers to draw along the length of the film. The continuous lines of the design will provide a continuity to the film, and other lines and shapes can be added to what will become individual frames. A preliminary planning chart can be printed or drawn showing the individual frames so that the children can develop a more controlled pattern on their film. Repeating the same shape on several consecutive frames will, of course, prolong its image on the screen. Making conscious use of this continuity, the students might even create pictorial films with developing and changing design patterns or more controlled story lines.

There is much room for creativity in film making without a camera. The earlier experiences in creating projected still images will result in better films. To produce these films in the classroom, the only physical requirement is a long flat surface on which the children can spread out the film as they work on it.

Making films using a movie camera will intrigue children, and movie cameras are now so simple to operate that they can be used by the quite young. If the equipment is available, children from about the age of eight onwards can produce their own movies. To begin with, discuss with them the preliminaries. Show them how to hold and handle the camera properly. Point out the basic requirements such as camera stability and slow panning so that the resulting film will be more satisfying.

The children should then work in groups to prepare a story line. Simple graphic representation of the story in the form of a wall chart will help in the actual filming later. Costumes, props, and sets may need to be gathered or created. In planning sets, the children can be introduced to the illusion of film making as they make houses that are one-sided or miniature models.

When the several tasks of the film have been assigned to different students, the actual filming can get underway. Either 8mm or 16mm film can be used, depending on the cameras and equipment available. There will be much excitement as children await the return of the processed film and many smiles as they see their work projected on the screen. Some editing will be necessary, and it should be determined by the children themselves. Sound can be added using a tape recorder that is then synchronized to the visual film.

Simple animation techniques do not require elaborate equipment, although a single-frame camera and mount will be needed. Children might model figures and objects out of modeling clay and add their own painted background. It is then easy to change the figures by reshaping them between each exposure of the film. Children will realize that changes in shape are made through gradual stages but will be greatly speeded up when seen on the screen. Cut-paper shapes can also be used for animated films: the shapes are arranged on a lighted table and moved about during the filming. This simple introduction will encourage children to explore further the magic of animated film making.

Whether done with or without a camera, films made by children will afford many new experiences and will help them to relate art to the environment they know.

Working with cameras and projectors is instructive as well as fun.
(Photo by George Saleeba)

Art can open our eyes to the world around us.

Afterthought

The foregoing chapters have presented an art program that is environment-oriented. We believe that such a program is the most positive and constructive one for the present time and for the foreseeable future because we believe that education as a whole must have as its overall purpose the integration of each individual into his society and his world.

Art, learning, and life are intertwined and inseparable. In the school curriculum, art is the one subject in which all others meet, for in the art class each child exercises his total understanding, awareness, and imagination creatively. Too, through art he learns to see and appreciate the world around him more fully.

To say that art teaching should be focused on the environment is only to propose that art be presented at every level in its most effective guise. It is not simply the development of skill in drawing and painting. It is more. In teaching art, the aim should be to lead each child to realize that art is the vital link between him and his world—his environment. Art helps him to see, to become sensitive to, to understand, to care about his world. It helps him to relate to his world and to express himself about it.

With awareness comes understanding. To see the world clearly is to discover relationships and design in time and space. In the natural world, children can learn to see the harmony and balance that is integral to the natural order. Withal, hopefully, they will come to appreciate order and plan.

Each child's own art work will mirror the world as he sees it with his "inner eye." Art teaching should encourage such expressions. At the same time, it should take every possible opportunity to expand the child's awareness and increase his sensitivity. Finally, it should result in greater understanding and a sense of involvement and responsibility.

To encourage a creative approach, then, to the person-environment relationship is the purpose of this book. What has been suggested in these pages is an idea for the orientation of an art curriculum. It is but a beginning and a challenge. The responsive, imaginative reader will see the implications and possibilities and develop a program accordingly.

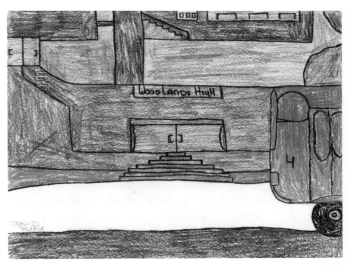

School expands the child's understanding of himself and his environment.

Bibliography

GENERAL ART EDUCATION

Greenberg, Pearl. *Art and Ideas for Young People.* New York: Van Nostrand Reinhold, 1970.

Greenberg, Pearl. *Children's Experiences in Art.* New York: Van Nostrand Reinhold, 1966.

Horn, George F. and Smith, Grace Sands. *Experiencing Art in the Elementary School.* Worcester, Mass.: Davis Publications, 1970.

Lidstone, John, Lewis, Stanley, and Brody, Sheldon. *Reinhold Visuals* (series of poster sets to teach awareness). New York: Van Nostrand Reinhold, 1968-1973

Rowland, Kurt. *Looking and Seeing Series.* New York: Van Nostrand Reinhold.

Shultz, Larry T. *Studio Art; A Resource for Artist-Teachers.* New York: Van Nostrand Reinhold, 1973.

Sproul, Adelaide. *With a Free Hand.* New York: Van Nostrand Reinhold, 1968.

DRAWING

Brommer, Gerald F. *Drawing: Ideas, Materials, and Techniques.* Worcester, Mass.: Davis Publications, 1972.

Kaupelis, Robert. *Learning to Draw.* New York: Watson-Guptill, 1966.

Laliberté, Norman and Mogelon, Alex. *Pastel, Charcoal, and Chalk Drawing.* New York: Van Nostrand Reinhold, 1973.

CLASSROOM ART PROJECTS

Airey, G., Bates, B., and Price, I. *New Ideas in Card and Paper Crafts.* New York: Van Nostrand Reinhold, 1973.

Andrew, Laye. *Creative Rubbings.* New York: Watson-Guptill, 1968.

Erickson, Janet and Sproul, Adelaide. *Print Making Without a Press.* New York: Van Nostrand Reinhold, 1973.

Green, Peter. *New Creative Print Making.* New York: Watson-Guptill, 1965.

Laliberté, Norman and Mogelon, Alex. *Masks, Face Coverings, and Headgear.* New York: Van Nostrand Reinhold, 1973.

Lidstone, John. *Building with Cardboard.* New York: Van Nostrand Reinhold, 1968.

Rogers, Edward and Sutcliff, Thomas. *Introducing Constructional Art.* New York: Watson-Guptill, 1971.

Rosenberg, Lilli. *Children Make Murals and Sculpture.* New York: Van Nostrand Reinhold, 1968.

Webb, Mary and Mayer, Mary Jane. *New Ways in Collage.* New York: Van Nostrand Reinhold, 1973.

USING MODERN MEDIA

Andersen, Yvonne. *Teaching Film Animation to Children.* New York: Van Nostrand Reinhold, 1971.

Cooke, Robert W. *Designing With Light on Paper and Film.* Worcester, Mass.: Davis Publications, 1969.

Holter, Patra. *Photography Without a Camera.* New York: Van Nostrand Reinhold, 1972.

Kennedy, Keith. *Film Making in Creative Teaching.* New York: Watson-Guptill, 1972.

Lidstone, John and McIntosh, Don. *Children as Film Makers.* New York: Van Nostrand Reinhold, 1970.

ART FROM THE ENVIRONMENT

D'Arbeloff, Natalie. *Designing With Natural Forms.* New York: Watson-Guptill, 1973.

Kampmann, Lothar. *Creating With Found Objects.* New York: Van Nostrand Reinhold, 1973.

Meilach, Dona and Hoor, Elvie. *Collage and Assemblage.* New York: Crown Publishers, 1973.

Moseley, Spencer, et al. *Crafts Design; An Illustrated Guide.* Belmont, Calif.: Wadsworth, 1962.

Palmer, Dennis. *Introducing Pattern.* New York: Watson-Guptill, 1970.

Rasmusen, Henry and Grant, Art. *Sculpture from Junk.* New York: Van Nostrand Reinhold, 1967.

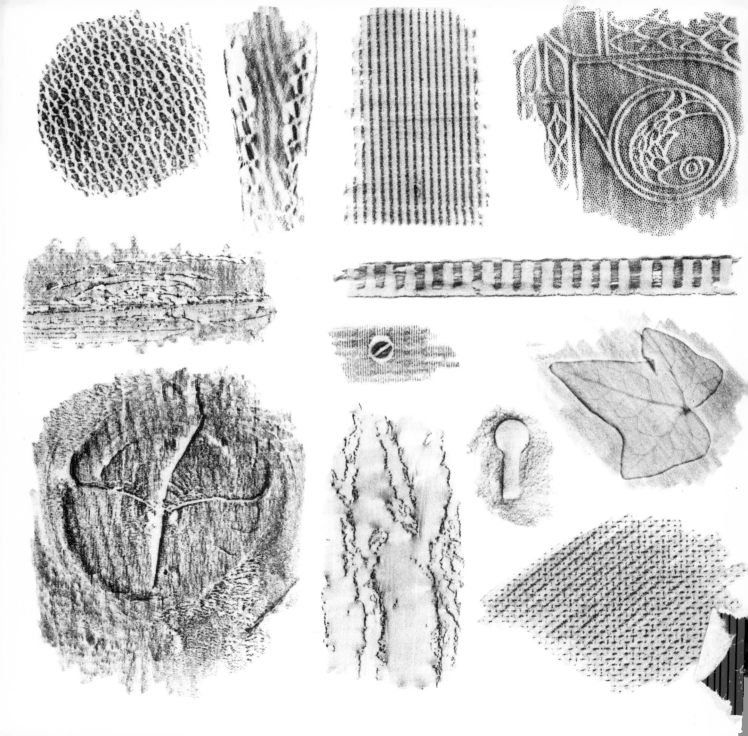

Index